How to Draw Mythical Creatures

MARC McBRIDE

SCHOLASTIC
SYDNEY AUCKLAND NEW YORK TORONTO LONDON MEXICO CITY
NEW DELHI HONG KONG BUENOS AIRES PUERTO RICO

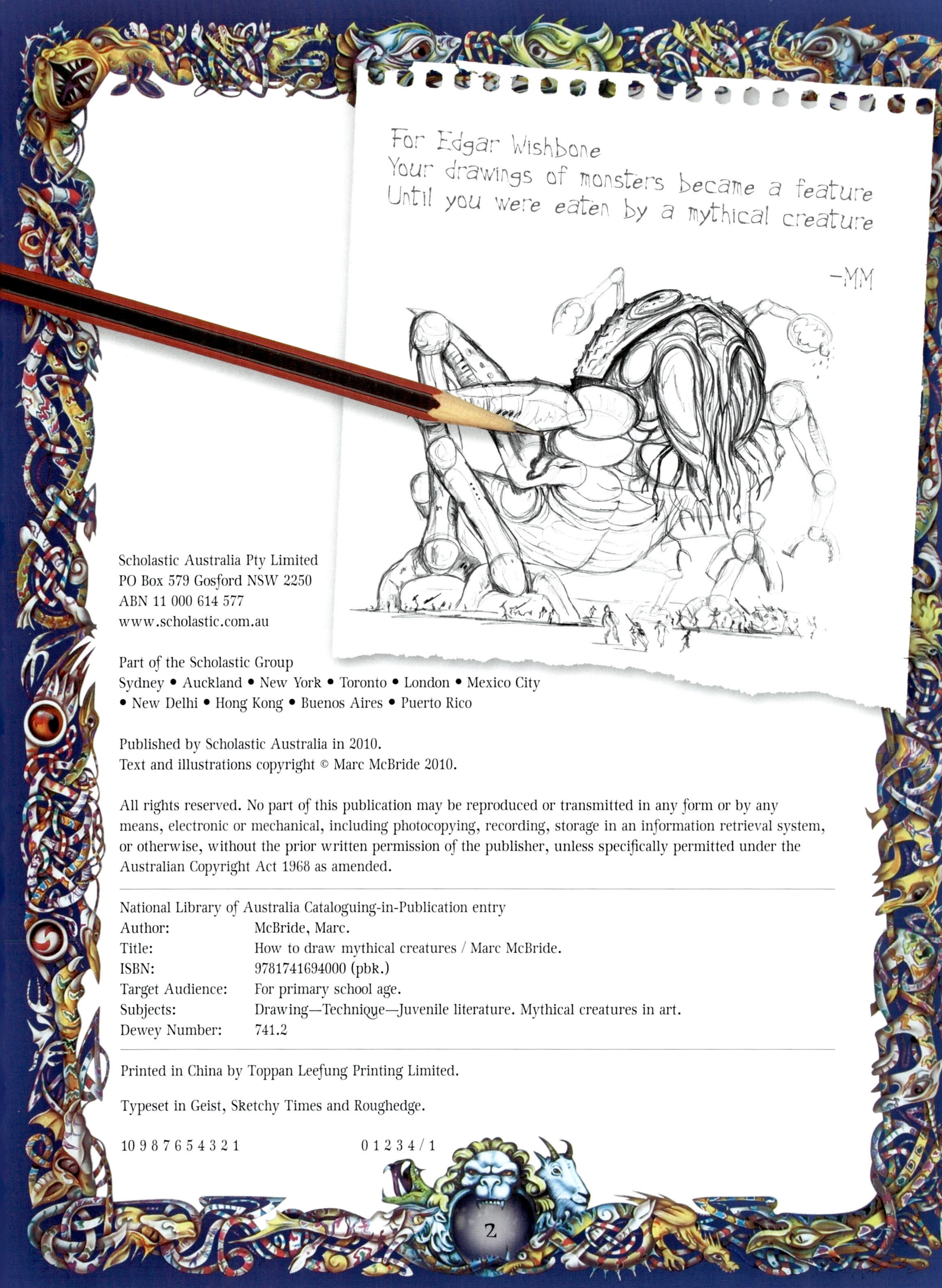

Scholastic Australia Pty Limited
PO Box 579 Gosford NSW 2250
ABN 11 000 614 577
www.scholastic.com.au

Part of the Scholastic Group
Sydney • Auckland • New York • Toronto • London • Mexico City
• New Delhi • Hong Kong • Buenos Aires • Puerto Rico

Published by Scholastic Australia in 2010.

National Library of Australia Cataloguing-in-Publication entry

Author:	McBride, Marc.
Title:	How to draw mythical creatures / Marc McBride.
ISBN:	9781741694000 (pbk.)
Target Audience:	For primary school age.
Subjects:	Drawing—Technique—Juvenile literature. Mythical creatures in art.
Dewey Number:	741.2

Printed in China by Toppan Leefung Printing Limited.

Typeset in Geist, Sketchy Times and Roughedge.

10 9 8 7 6 5 4 3 2 1 0 1 2 3 4 / 1

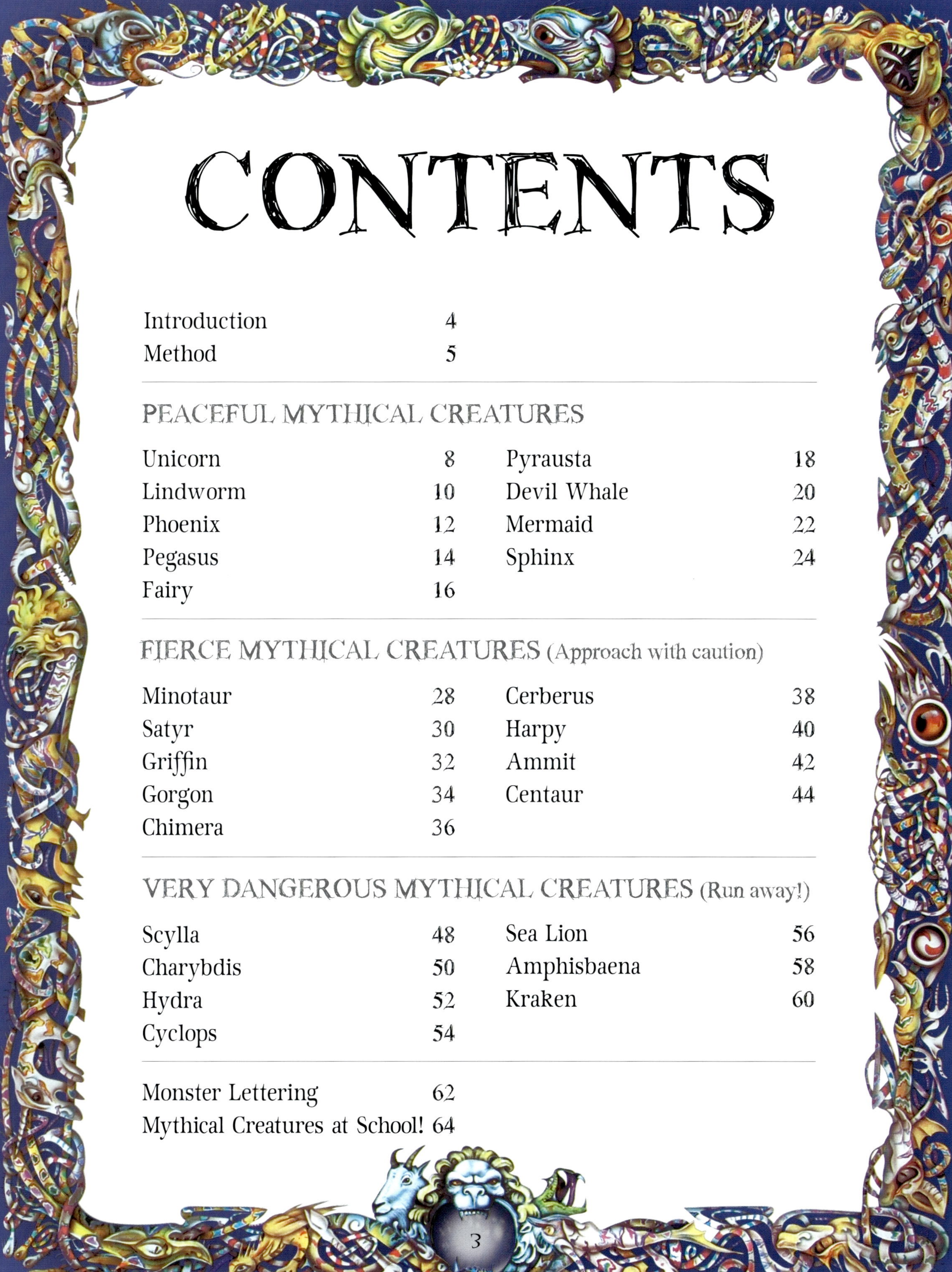

CONTENTS

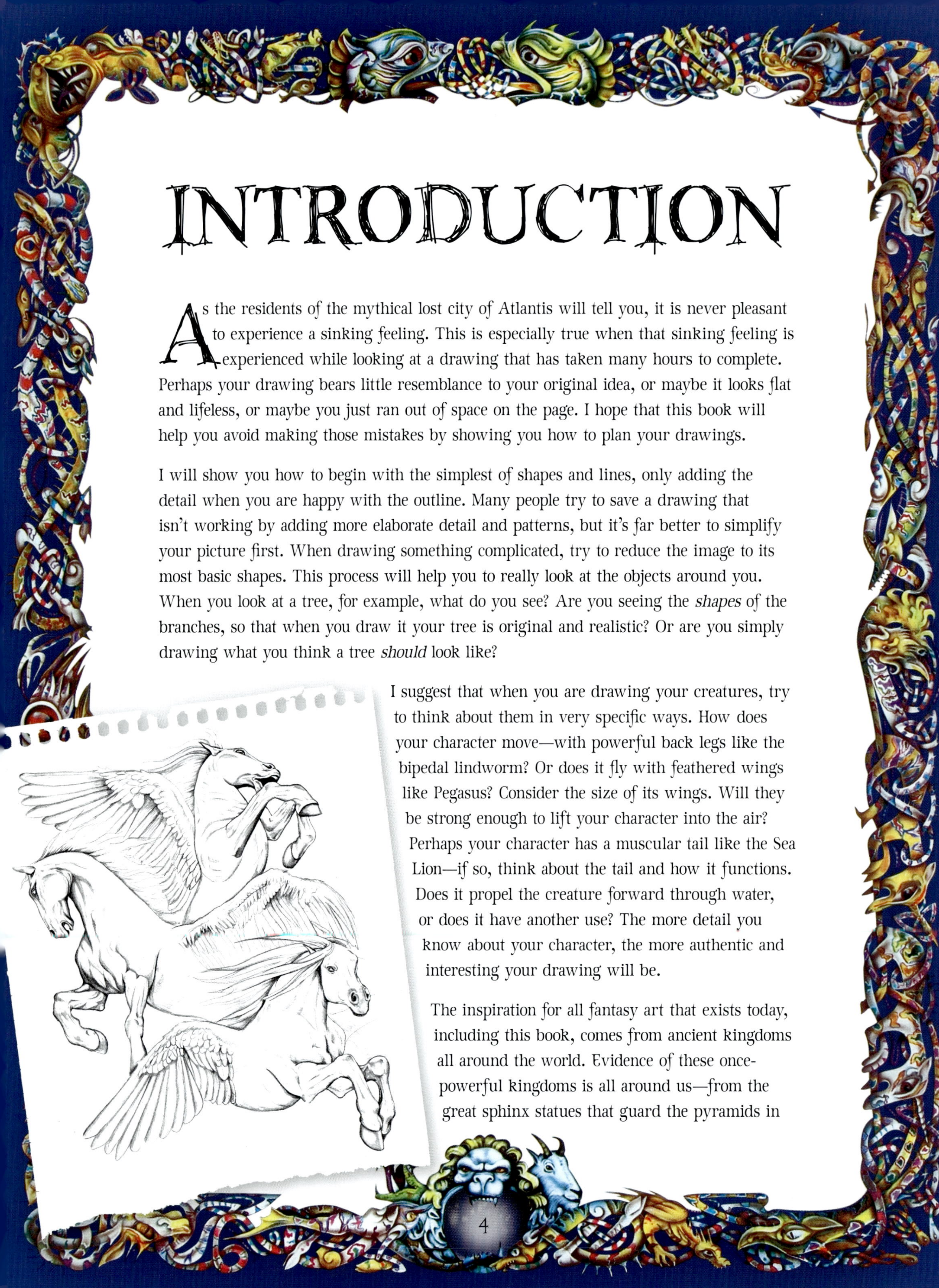

INTRODUCTION

As the residents of the mythical lost city of Atlantis will tell you, it is never pleasant to experience a sinking feeling. This is especially true when that sinking feeling is experienced while looking at a drawing that has taken many hours to complete. Perhaps your drawing bears little resemblance to your original idea, or maybe it looks flat and lifeless, or maybe you just ran out of space on the page. I hope that this book will help you avoid making those mistakes by showing you how to plan your drawings.

I will show you how to begin with the simplest of shapes and lines, only adding the detail when you are happy with the outline. Many people try to save a drawing that isn't working by adding more elaborate detail and patterns, but it's far better to simplify your picture first. When drawing something complicated, try to reduce the image to its most basic shapes. This process will help you to really look at the objects around you. When you look at a tree, for example, what do you see? Are you seeing the *shapes* of the branches, so that when you draw it your tree is original and realistic? Or are you simply drawing what you think a tree *should* look like?

I suggest that when you are drawing your creatures, try to think about them in very specific ways. How does your character move—with powerful back legs like the bipedal lindworm? Or does it fly with feathered wings like Pegasus? Consider the size of its wings. Will they be strong enough to lift your character into the air? Perhaps your character has a muscular tail like the Sea Lion—if so, think about the tail and how it functions. Does it propel the creature forward through water, or does it have another use? The more detail you know about your character, the more authentic and interesting your drawing will be.

The inspiration for all fantasy art that exists today, including this book, comes from ancient kingdoms all around the world. Evidence of these once-powerful kingdoms is all around us—from the great sphinx statues that guard the pyramids in

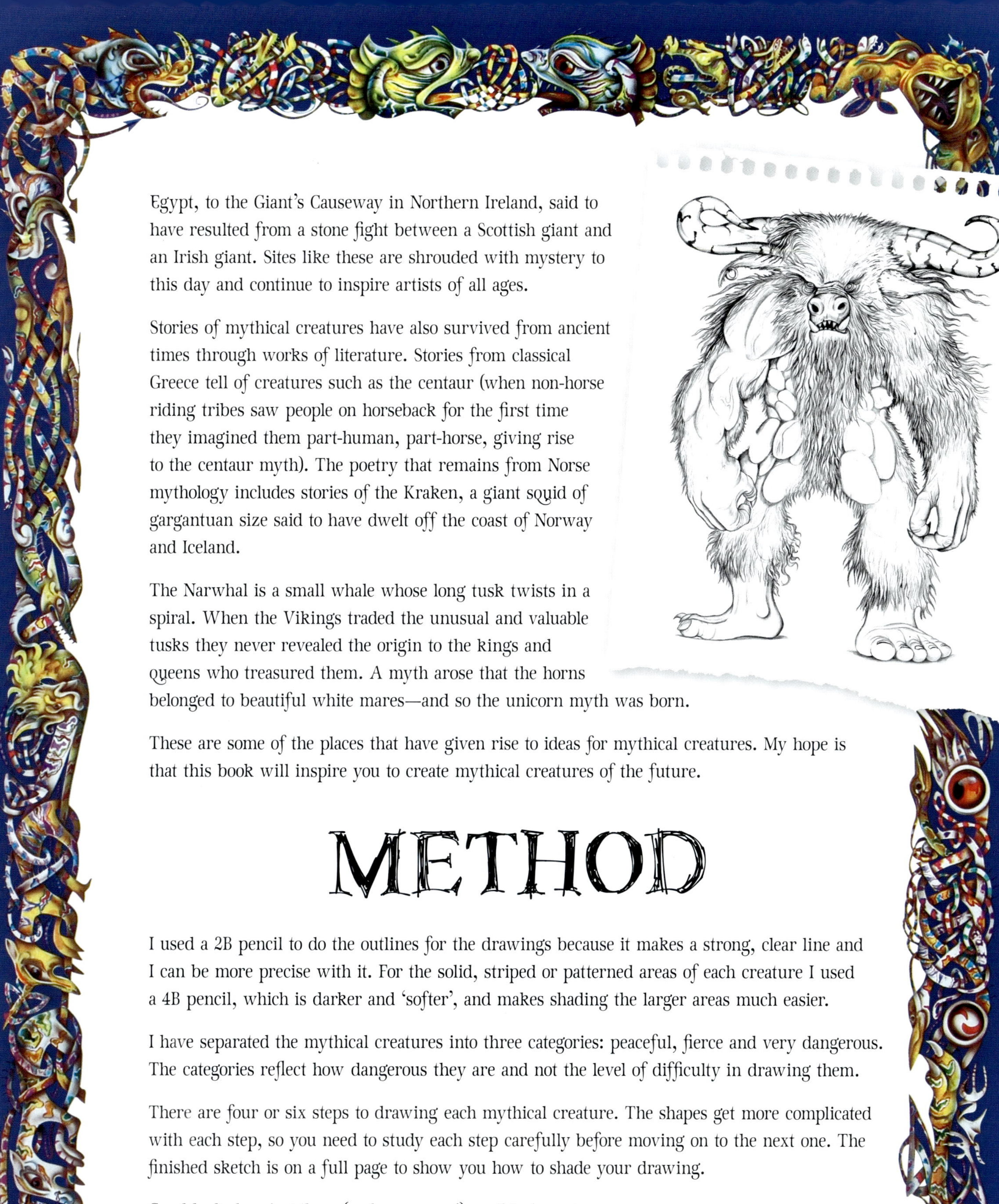

Egypt, to the Giant's Causeway in Northern Ireland, said to have resulted from a stone fight between a Scottish giant and an Irish giant. Sites like these are shrouded with mystery to this day and continue to inspire artists of all ages.

Stories of mythical creatures have also survived from ancient times through works of literature. Stories from classical Greece tell of creatures such as the centaur (when non-horse riding tribes saw people on horseback for the first time they imagined them part-human, part-horse, giving rise to the centaur myth). The poetry that remains from Norse mythology includes stories of the Kraken, a giant squid of gargantuan size said to have dwelt off the coast of Norway and Iceland.

The Narwhal is a small whale whose long tusk twists in a spiral. When the Vikings traded the unusual and valuable tusks they never revealed the origin to the kings and queens who treasured them. A myth arose that the horns belonged to beautiful white mares—and so the unicorn myth was born.

These are some of the places that have given rise to ideas for mythical creatures. My hope is that this book will inspire you to create mythical creatures of the future.

METHOD

I used a 2B pencil to do the outlines for the drawings because it makes a strong, clear line and I can be more precise with it. For the solid, striped or patterned areas of each creature I used a 4B pencil, which is darker and 'softer', and makes shading the larger areas much easier.

I have separated the mythical creatures into three categories: peaceful, fierce and very dangerous. The categories reflect how dangerous they are and not the level of difficulty in drawing them.

There are four or six steps to drawing each mythical creature. The shapes get more complicated with each step, so you need to study each step carefully before moving on to the next one. The finished sketch is on a full page to show you how to shade your drawing.

Good luck drawing these (and your own!) mythical creatures.

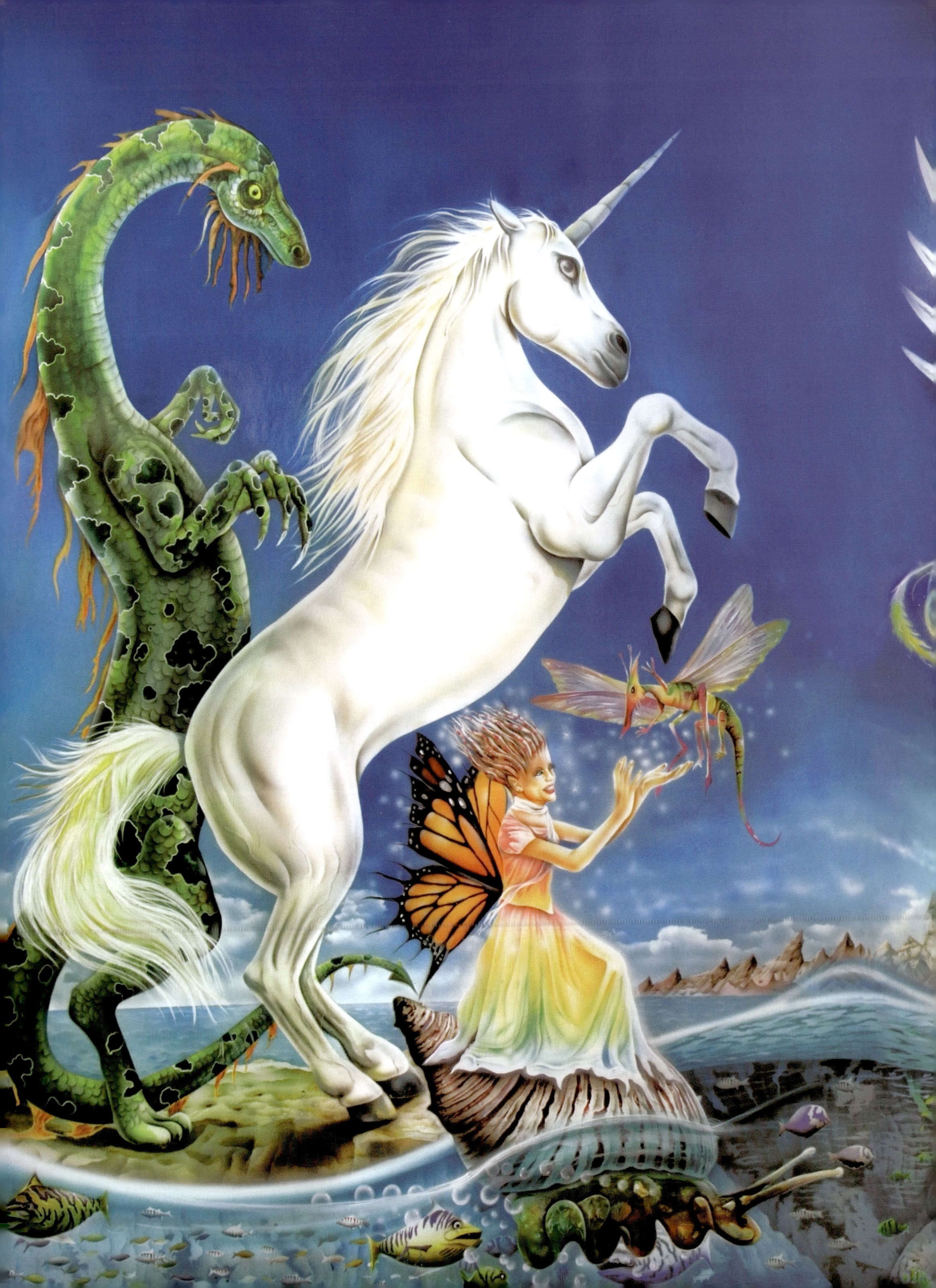

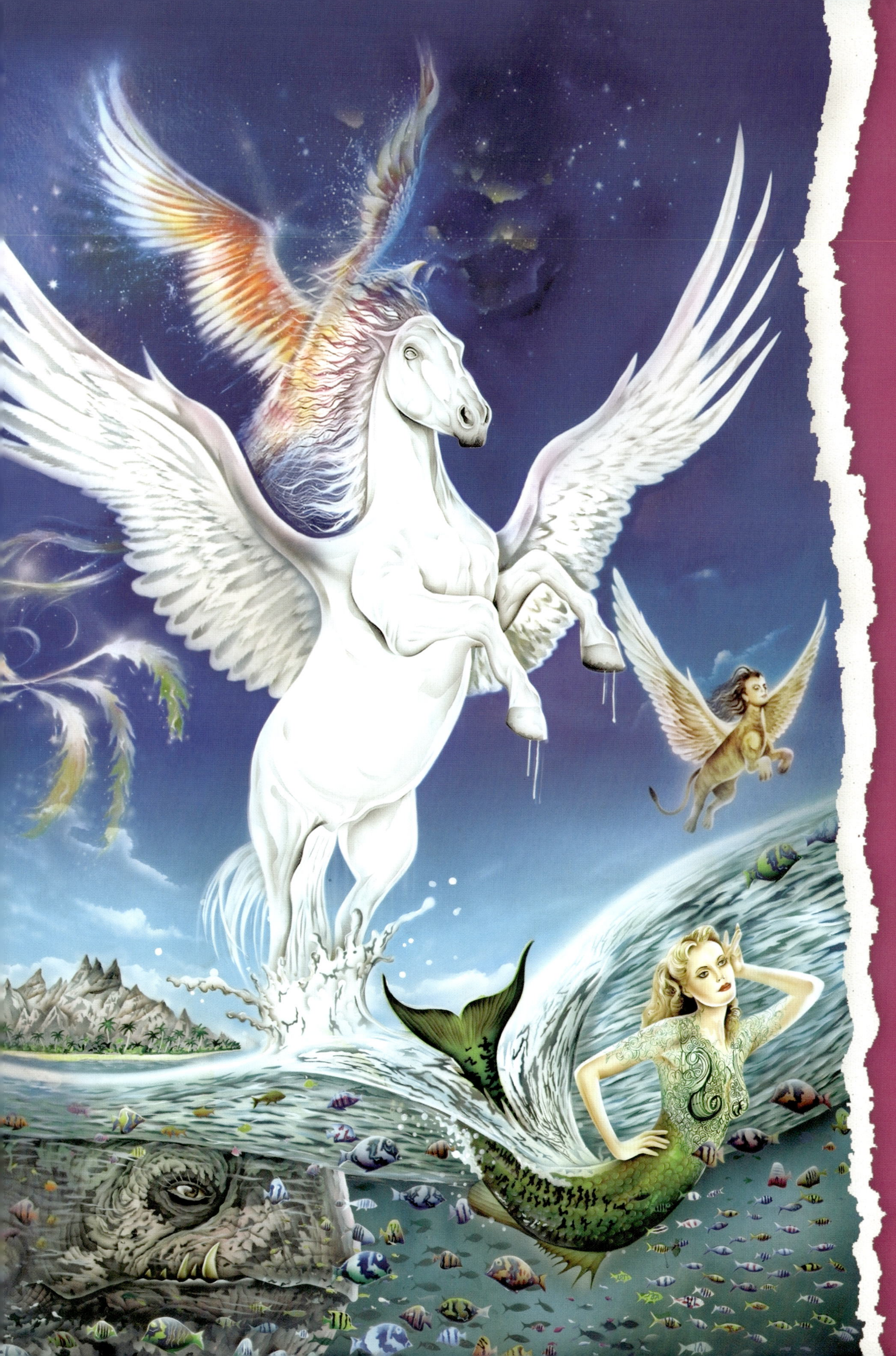

PEACEFUL MYTHICAL CREATURES

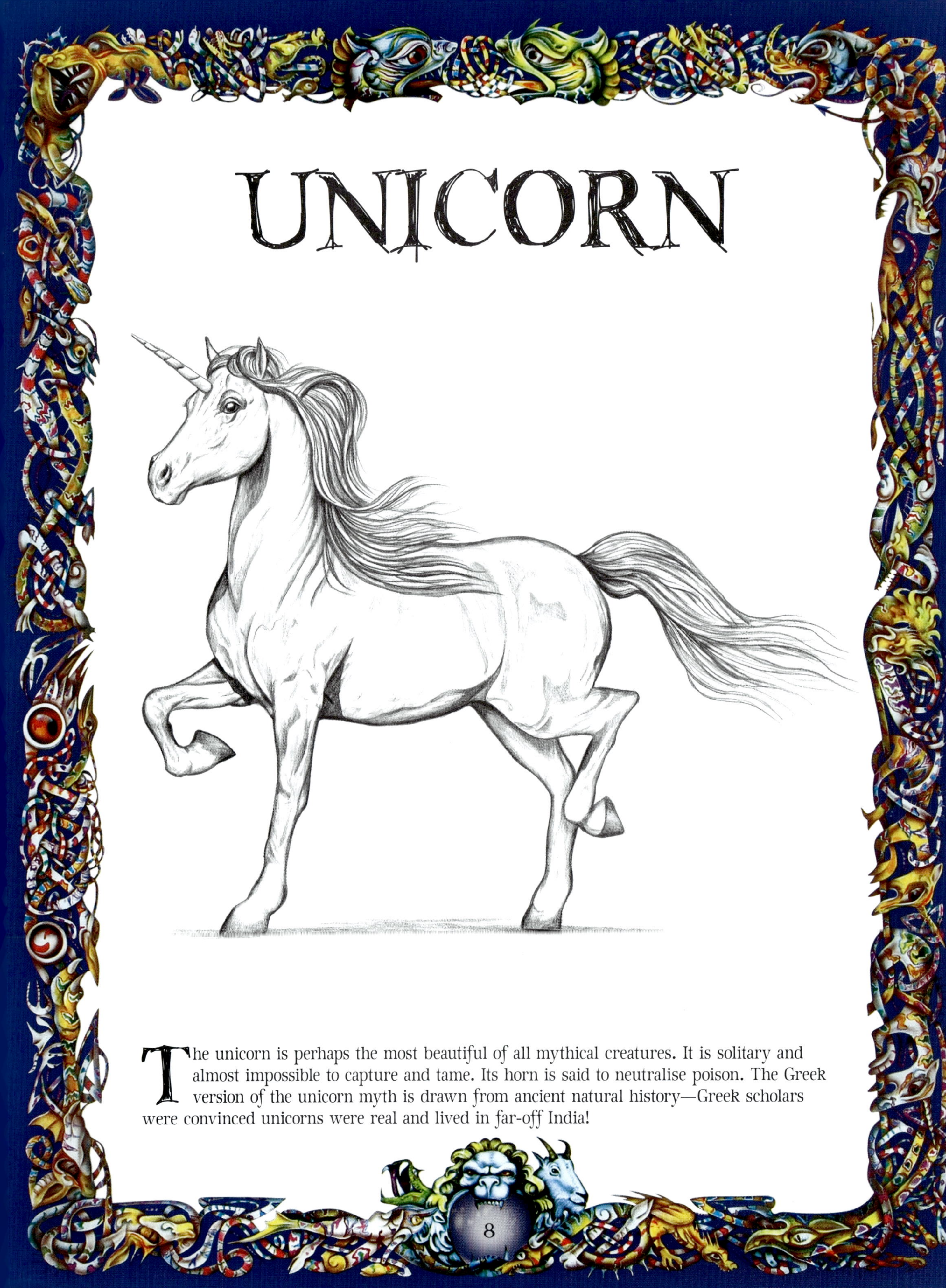

UNICORN

The unicorn is perhaps the most beautiful of all mythical creatures. It is solitary and almost impossible to capture and tame. Its horn is said to neutralise poison. The Greek version of the unicorn myth is drawn from ancient natural history—Greek scholars were convinced unicorns were real and lived in far-off India!

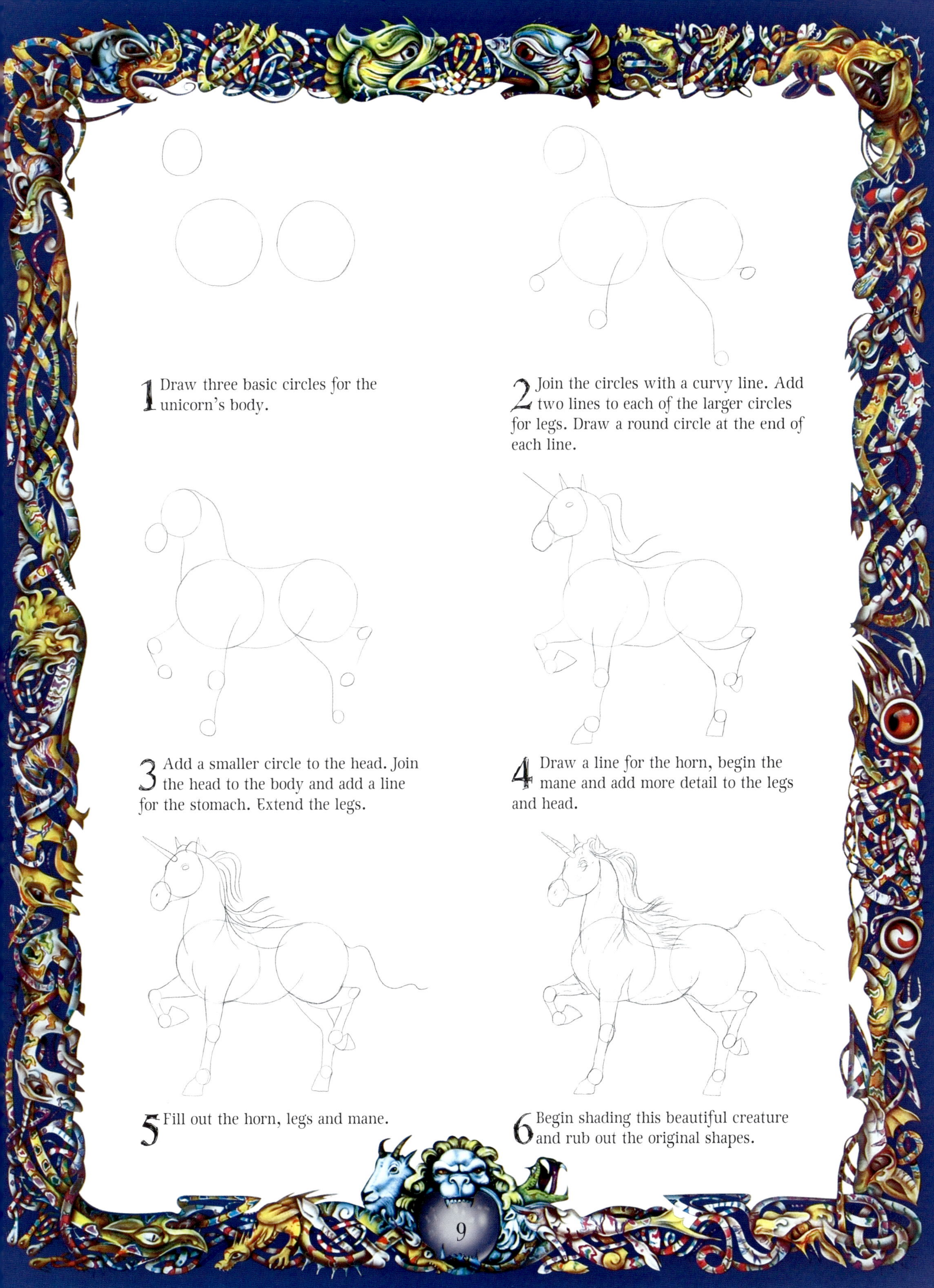

1 Draw three basic circles for the unicorn's body.

2 Join the circles with a curvy line. Add two lines to each of the larger circles for legs. Draw a round circle at the end of each line.

3 Add a smaller circle to the head. Join the head to the body and add a line for the stomach. Extend the legs.

4 Draw a line for the horn, begin the mane and add more detail to the legs and head.

5 Fill out the horn, legs and mane.

6 Begin shading this beautiful creature and rub out the original shapes.

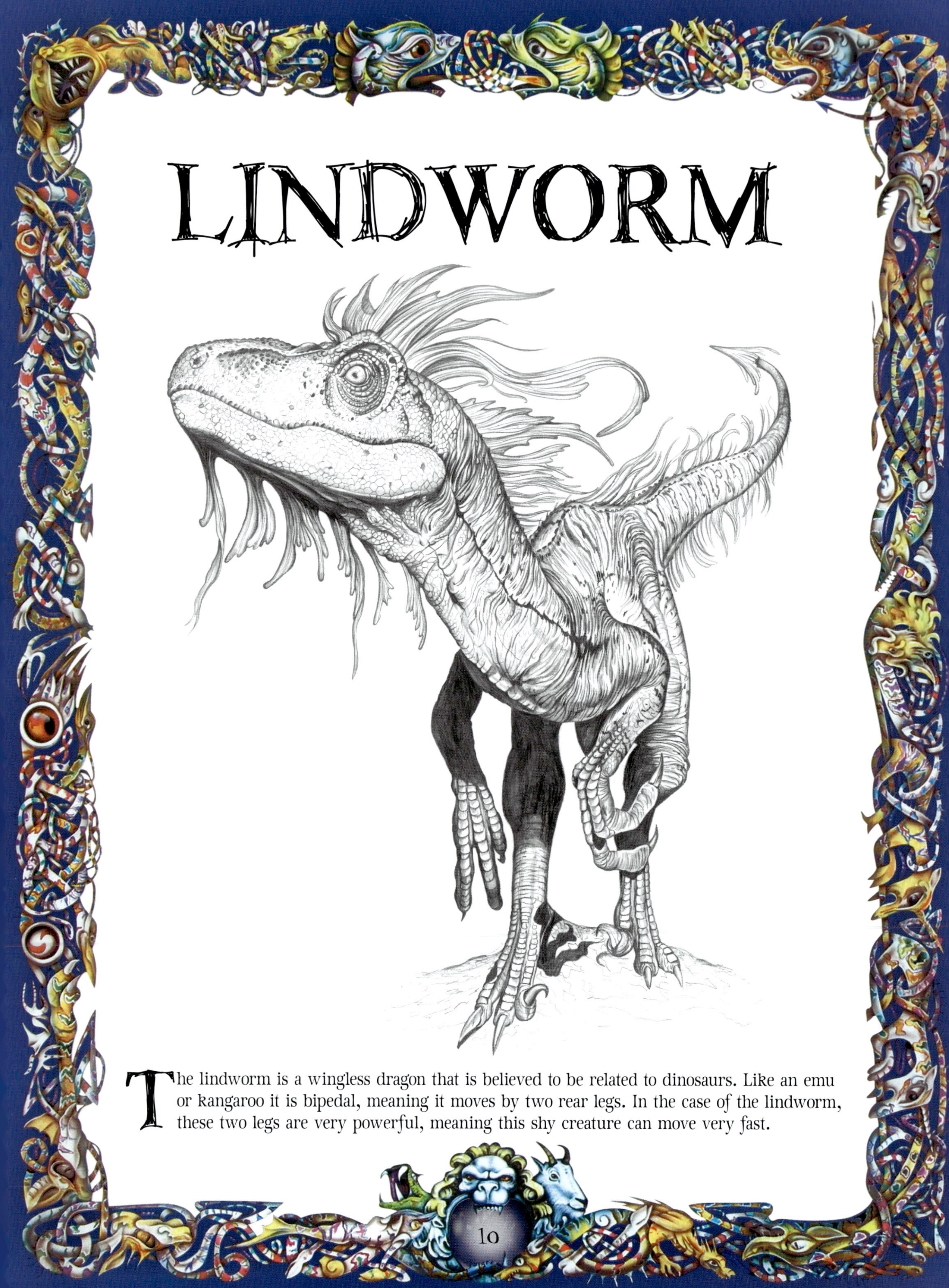

LINDWORM

The lindworm is a wingless dragon that is believed to be related to dinosaurs. Like an emu or kangaroo it is bipedal, meaning it moves by two rear legs. In the case of the lindworm, these two legs are very powerful, meaning this shy creature can move very fast.

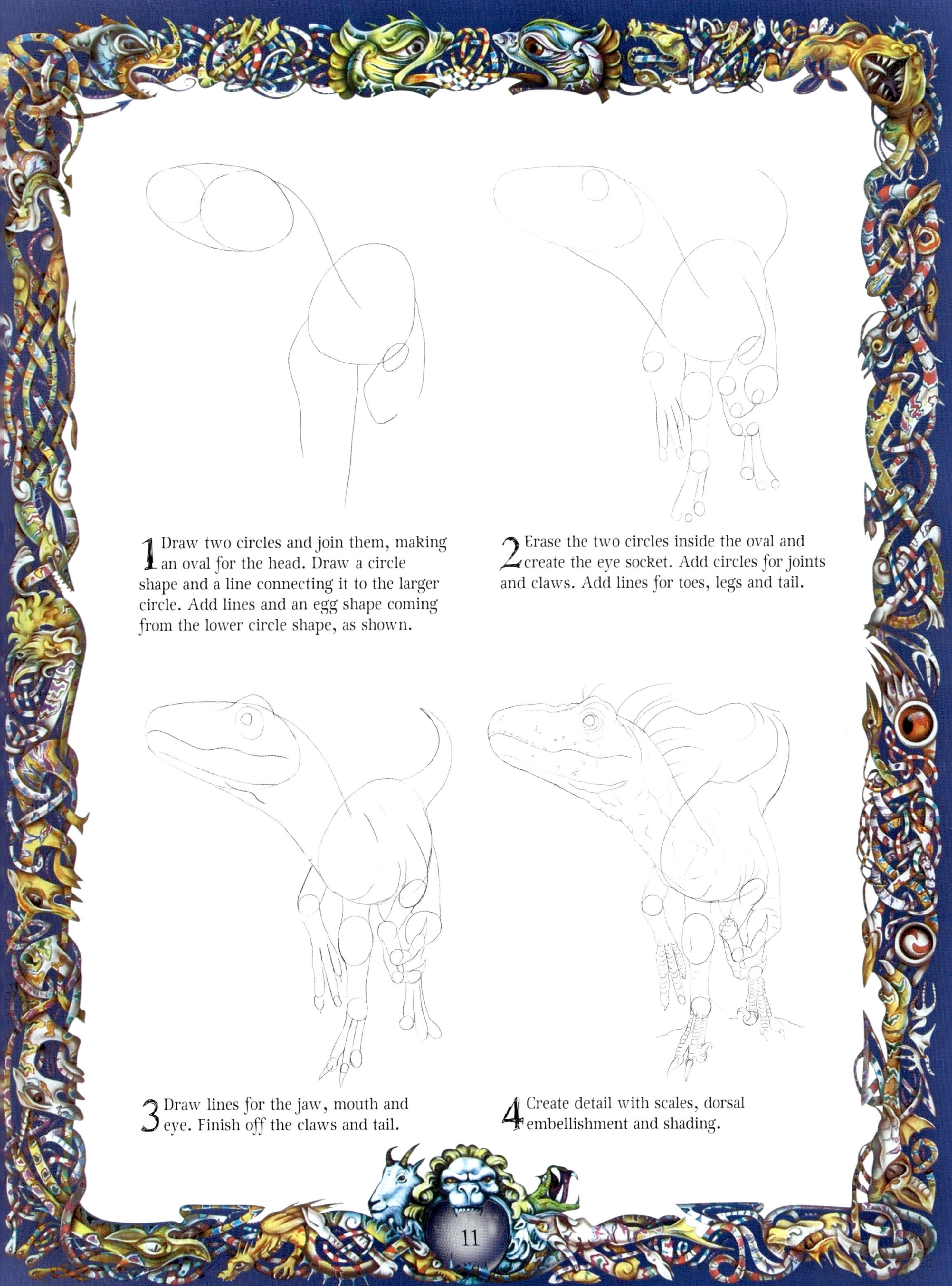

1 Draw two circles and join them, making an oval for the head. Draw a circle shape and a line connecting it to the larger circle. Add lines and an egg shape coming from the lower circle shape, as shown.

2 Erase the two circles inside the oval and create the eye socket. Add circles for joints and claws. Add lines for toes, legs and tail.

3 Draw lines for the jaw, mouth and eye. Finish off the claws and tail.

4 Create detail with scales, dorsal embellishment and shading.

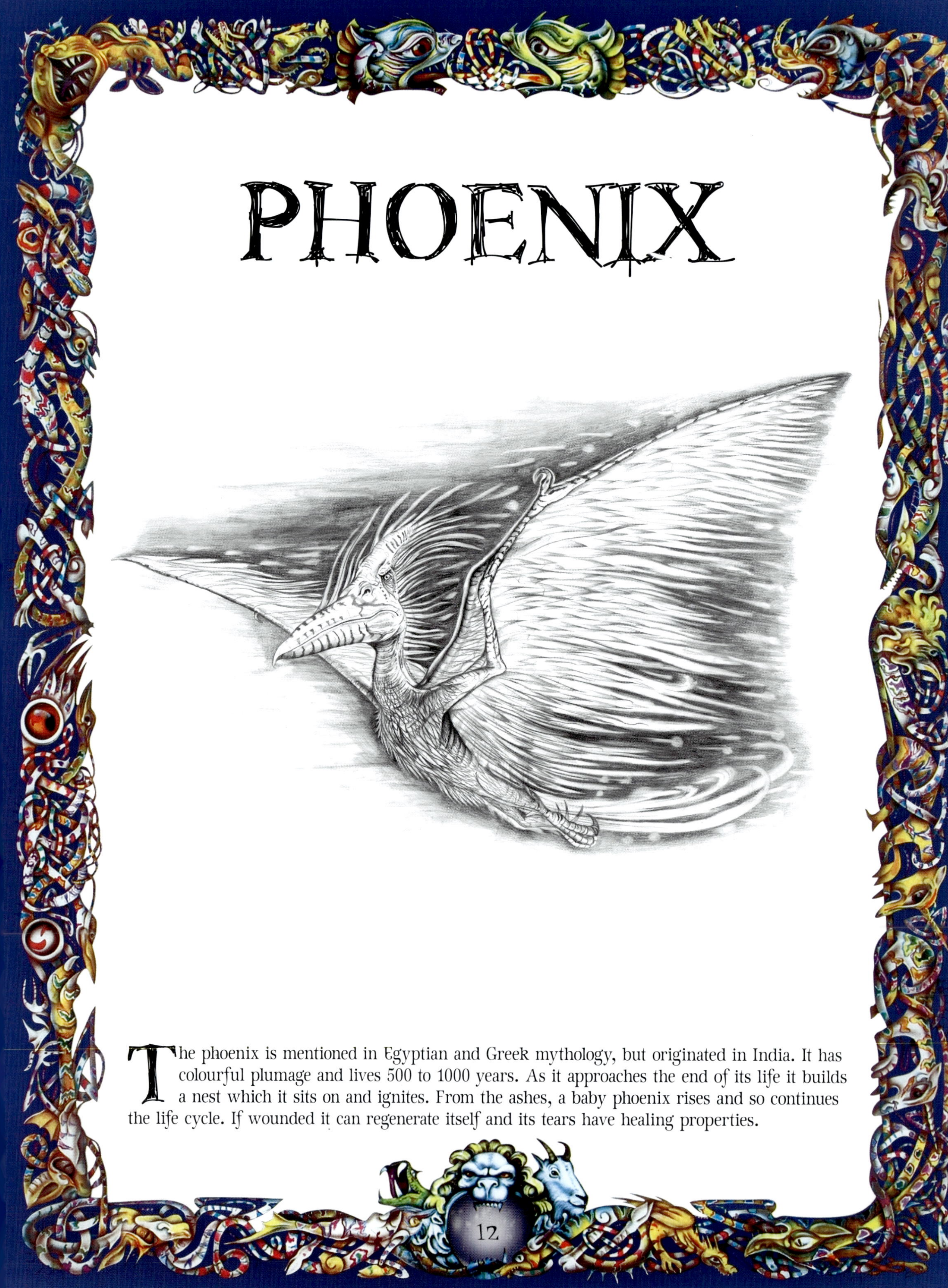

PHOENIX

The phoenix is mentioned in Egyptian and Greek mythology, but originated in India. It has colourful plumage and lives 500 to 1000 years. As it approaches the end of its life it builds a nest which it sits on and ignites. From the ashes, a baby phoenix rises and so continues the life cycle. If wounded it can regenerate itself and its tears have healing properties.

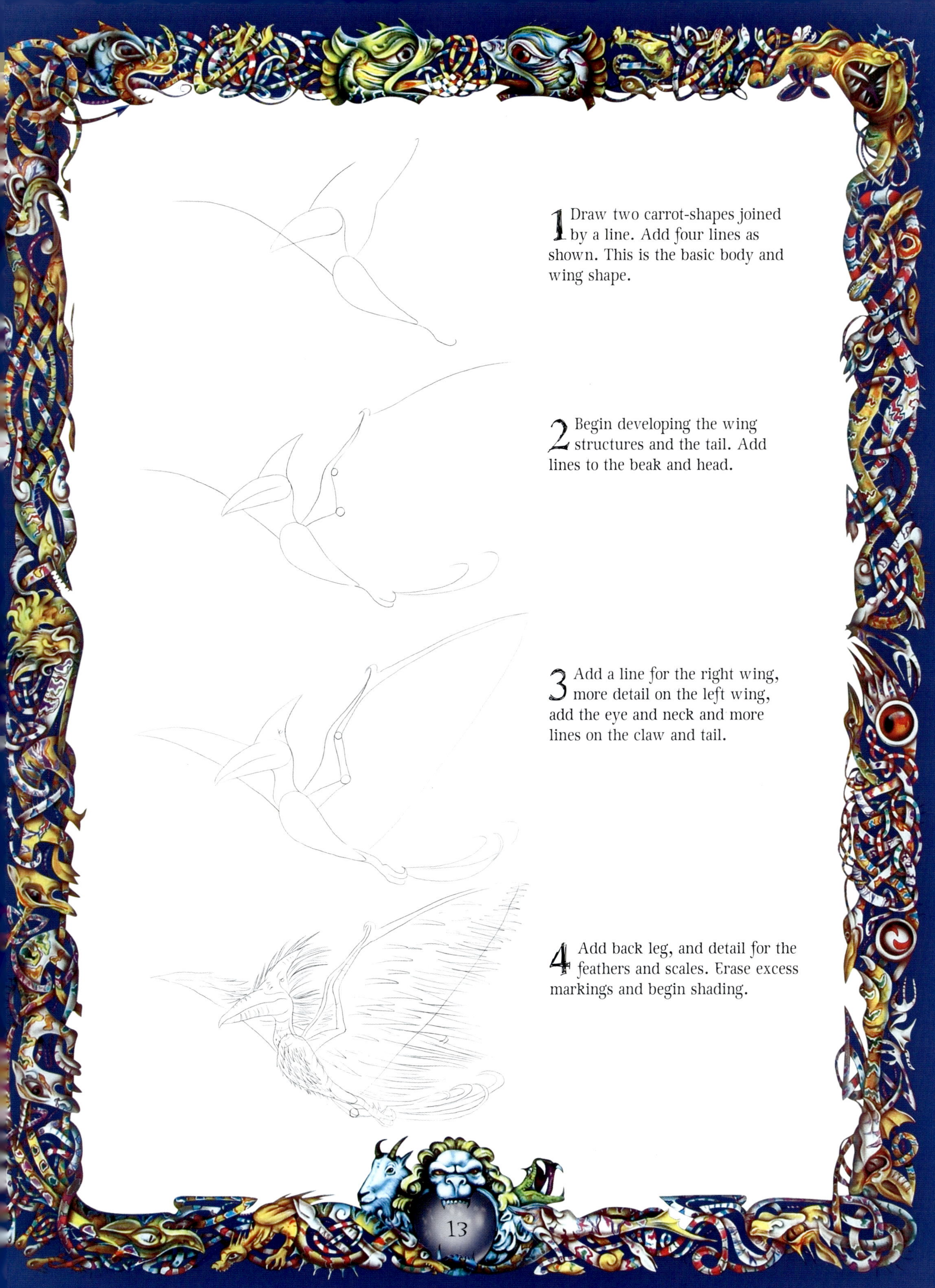

1 Draw two carrot-shapes joined by a line. Add four lines as shown. This is the basic body and wing shape.

2 Begin developing the wing structures and the tail. Add lines to the beak and head.

3 Add a line for the right wing, more detail on the left wing, add the eye and neck and more lines on the claw and tail.

4 Add back leg, and detail for the feathers and scales. Erase excess markings and begin shading.

PEGASUS

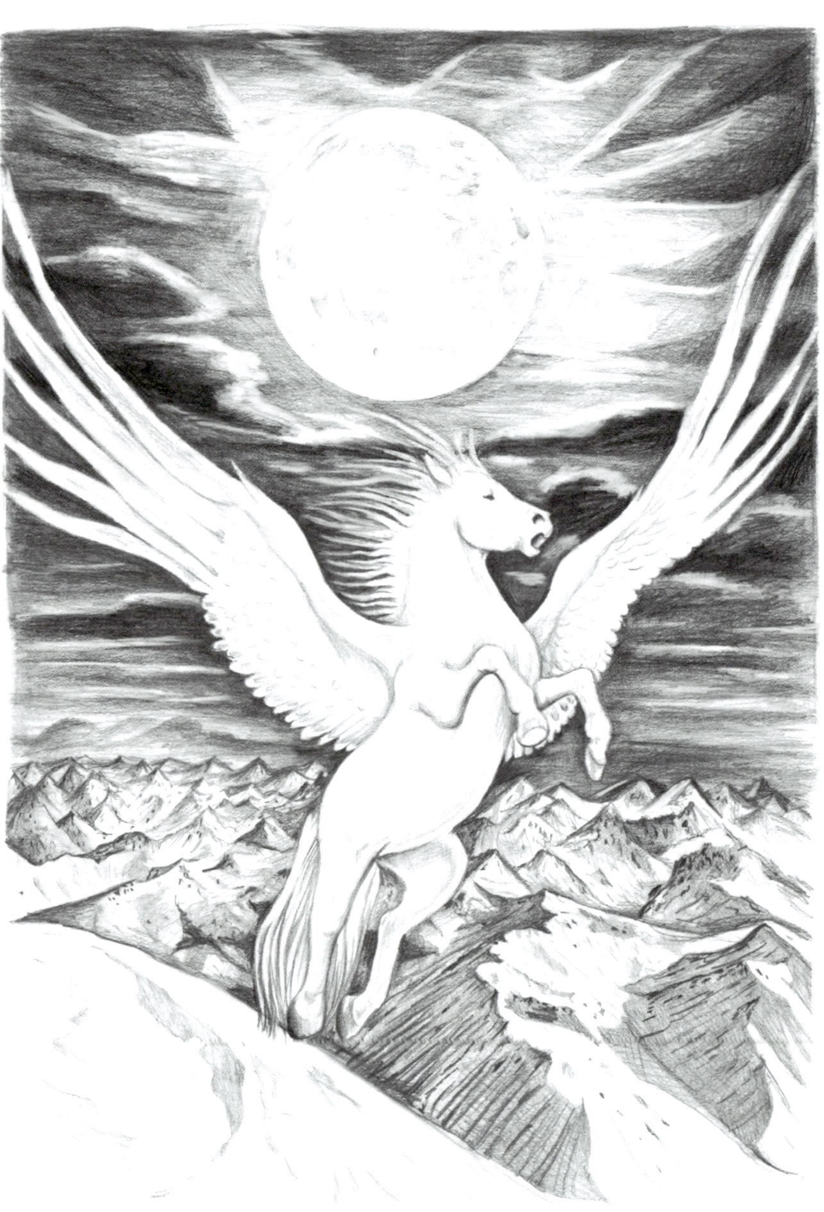

Pegasus is said to mean 'well' and wherever its hoof strikes the Earth a spring bursts forth. Others say it means 'lightning', as it carries thunderbolts. The winged horse appears in many stories in Greek mythology, where he is said to have helped defeat the Chimera (p36).

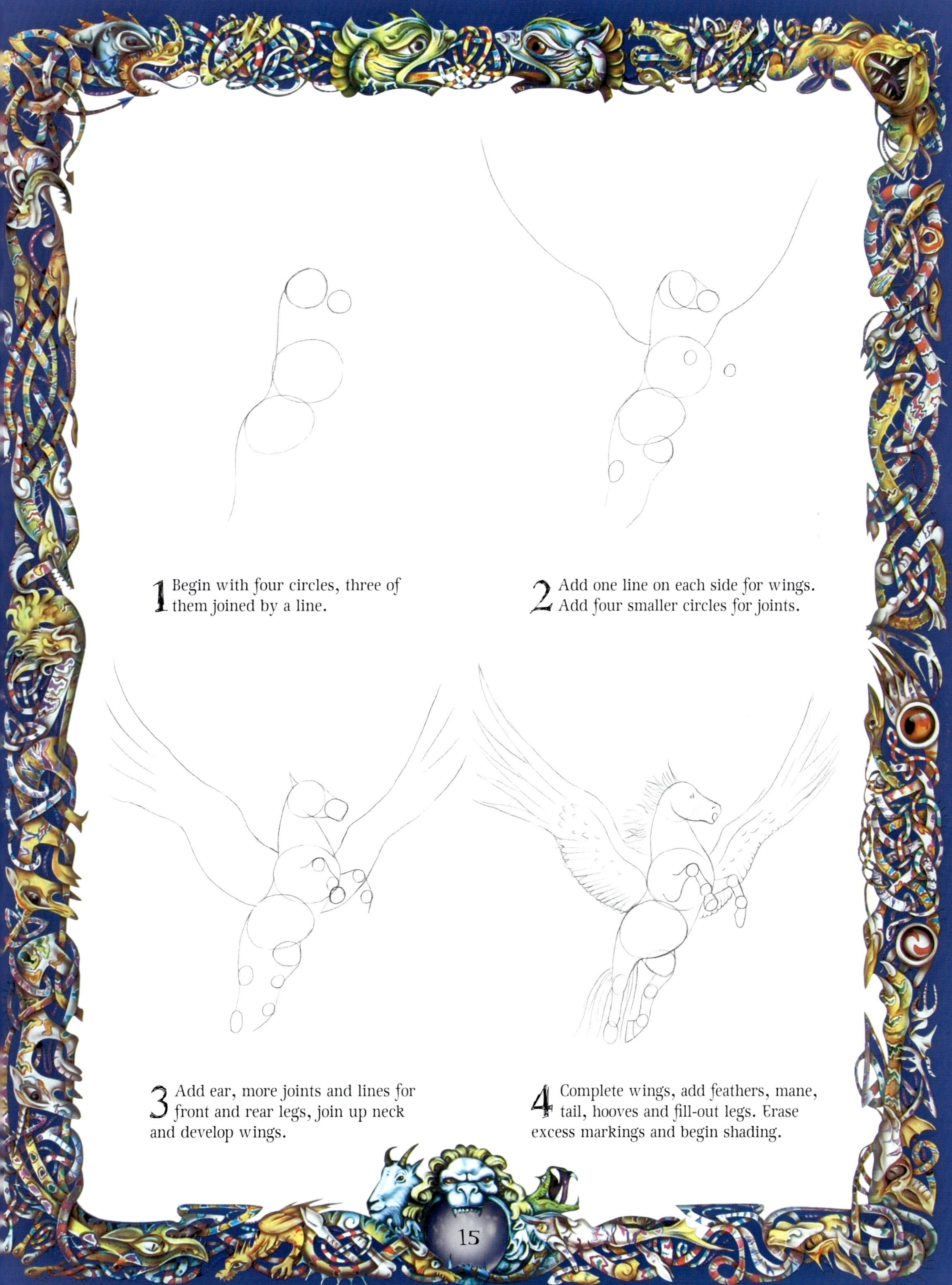

1 Begin with four circles, three of them joined by a line.

2 Add one line on each side for wings. Add four smaller circles for joints.

3 Add ear, more joints and lines for front and rear legs, join up neck and develop wings.

4 Complete wings, add feathers, mane, tail, hooves and fill-out legs. Erase excess markings and begin shading.

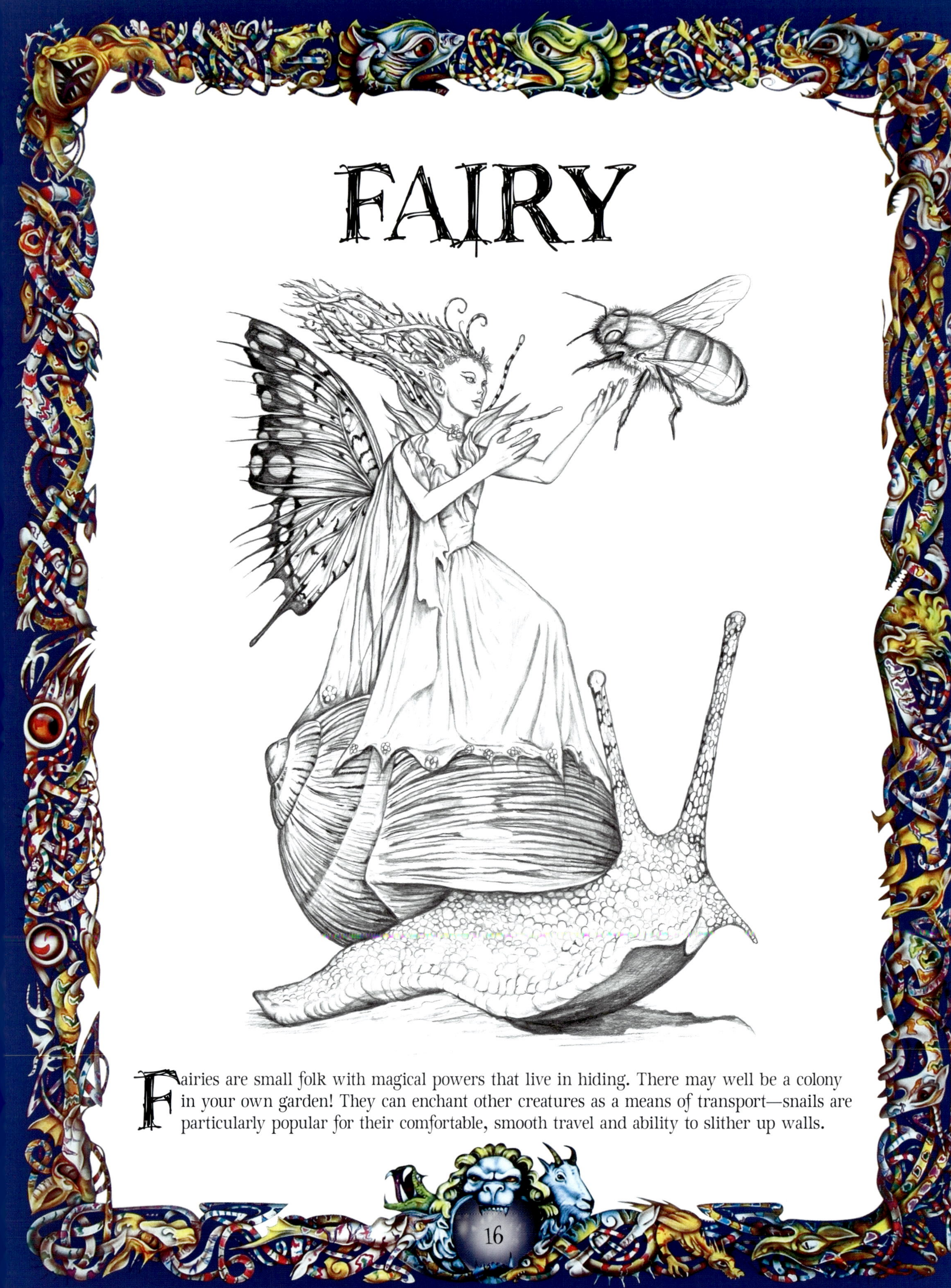

FAIRY

Fairies are small folk with magical powers that live in hiding. There may well be a colony in your own garden! They can enchant other creatures as a means of transport—snails are particularly popular for their comfortable, smooth travel and ability to slither up walls.

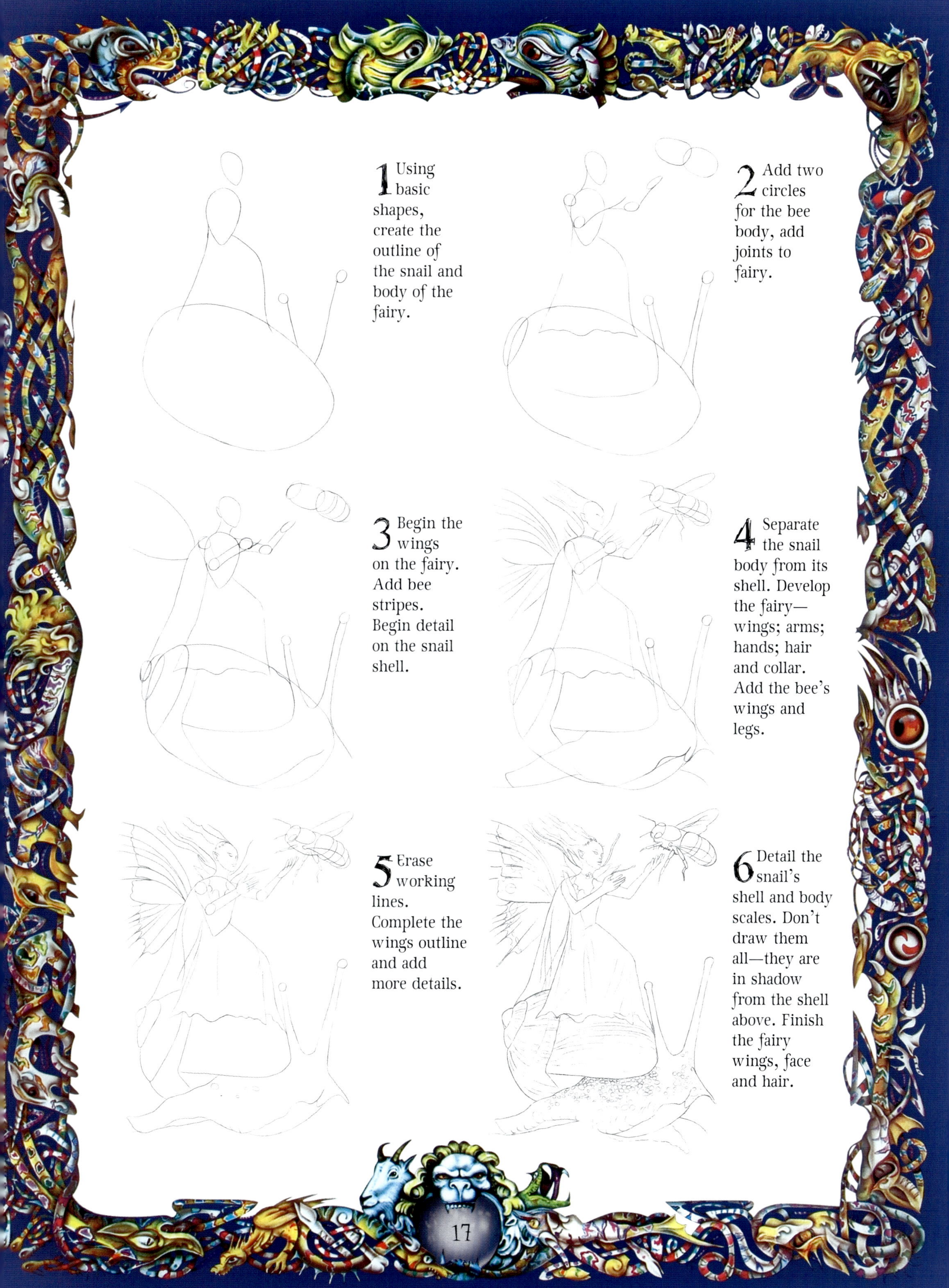

1 Using basic shapes, create the outline of the snail and body of the fairy.

2 Add two circles for the bee body, add joints to fairy.

3 Begin the wings on the fairy. Add bee stripes. Begin detail on the snail shell.

4 Separate the snail body from its shell. Develop the fairy—wings; arms; hands; hair and collar. Add the bee's wings and legs.

5 Erase working lines. Complete the wings outline and add more details.

6 Detail the snail's shell and body scales. Don't draw them all—they are in shadow from the shell above. Finish the fairy wings, face and hair.

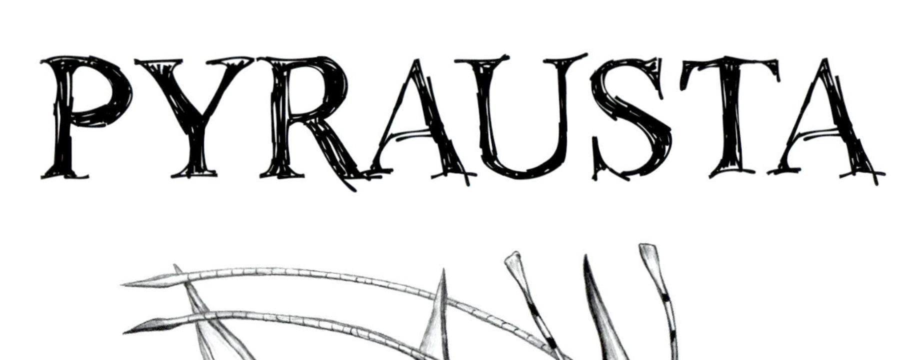

PYRAUSTA

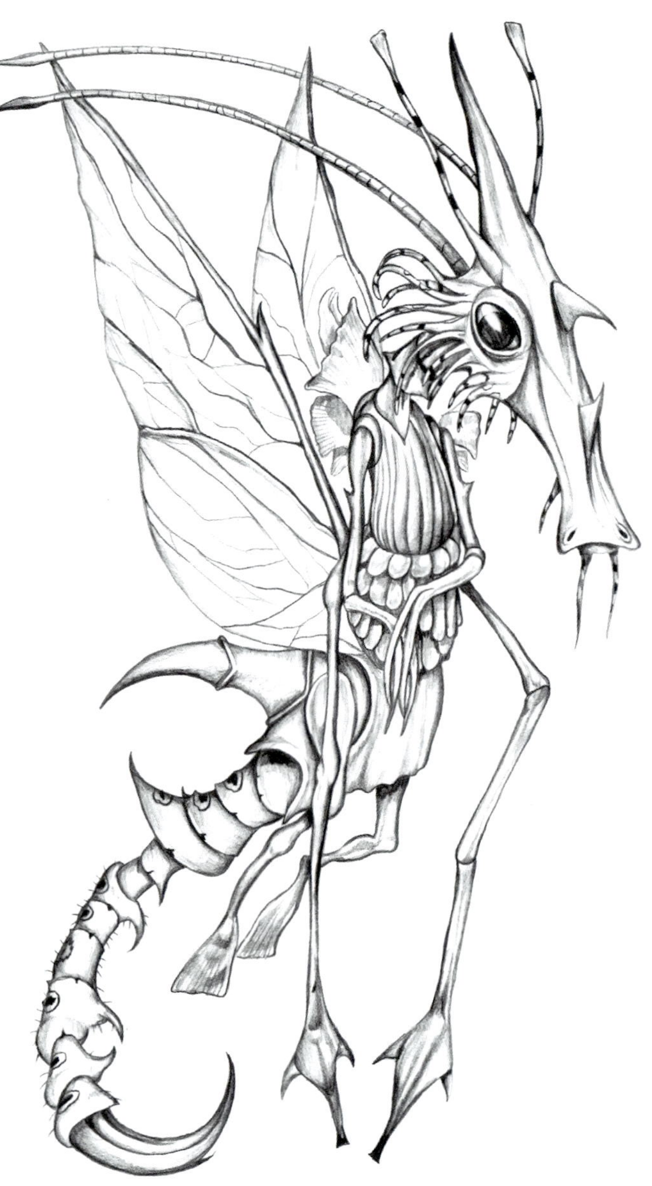

Pyrausta is a dragon-like insect. Extremely rare, it is the one creature in this book that may in fact be real. It has been known to borrow things such as pencils, sharpeners and erasers. They mostly forget to give them back for some time until finally returning them to the original place from which they went missing!

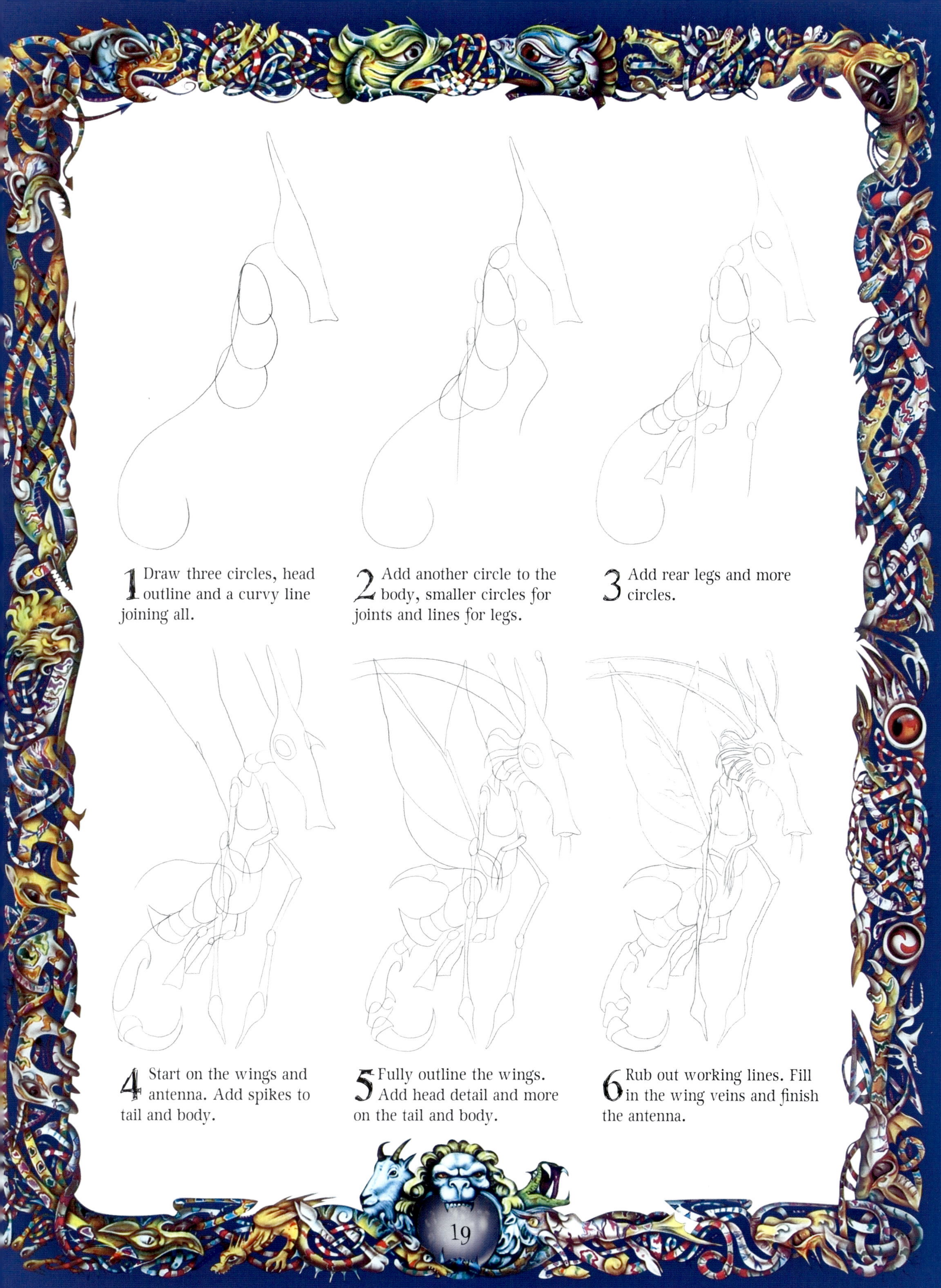

1 Draw three circles, head outline and a curvy line joining all.

2 Add another circle to the body, smaller circles for joints and lines for legs.

3 Add rear legs and more circles.

4 Start on the wings and antenna. Add spikes to tail and body.

5 Fully outline the wings. Add head detail and more on the tail and body.

6 Rub out working lines. Fill in the wing veins and finish the antenna.

DEVIL WHALE

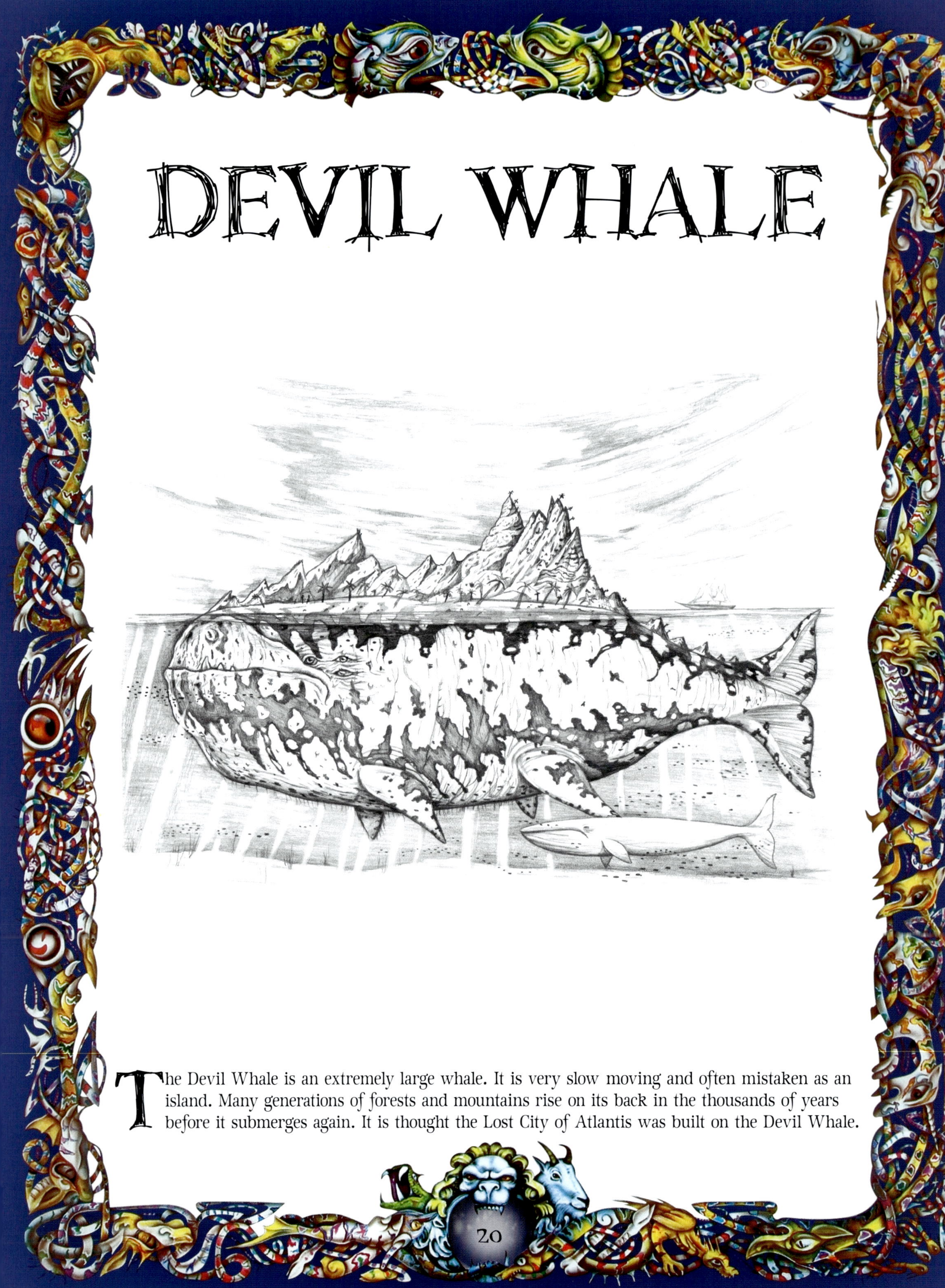

The Devil Whale is an extremely large whale. It is very slow moving and often mistaken as an island. Many generations of forests and mountains rise on its back in the thousands of years before it submerges again. It is thought the Lost City of Atlantis was built on the Devil Whale.

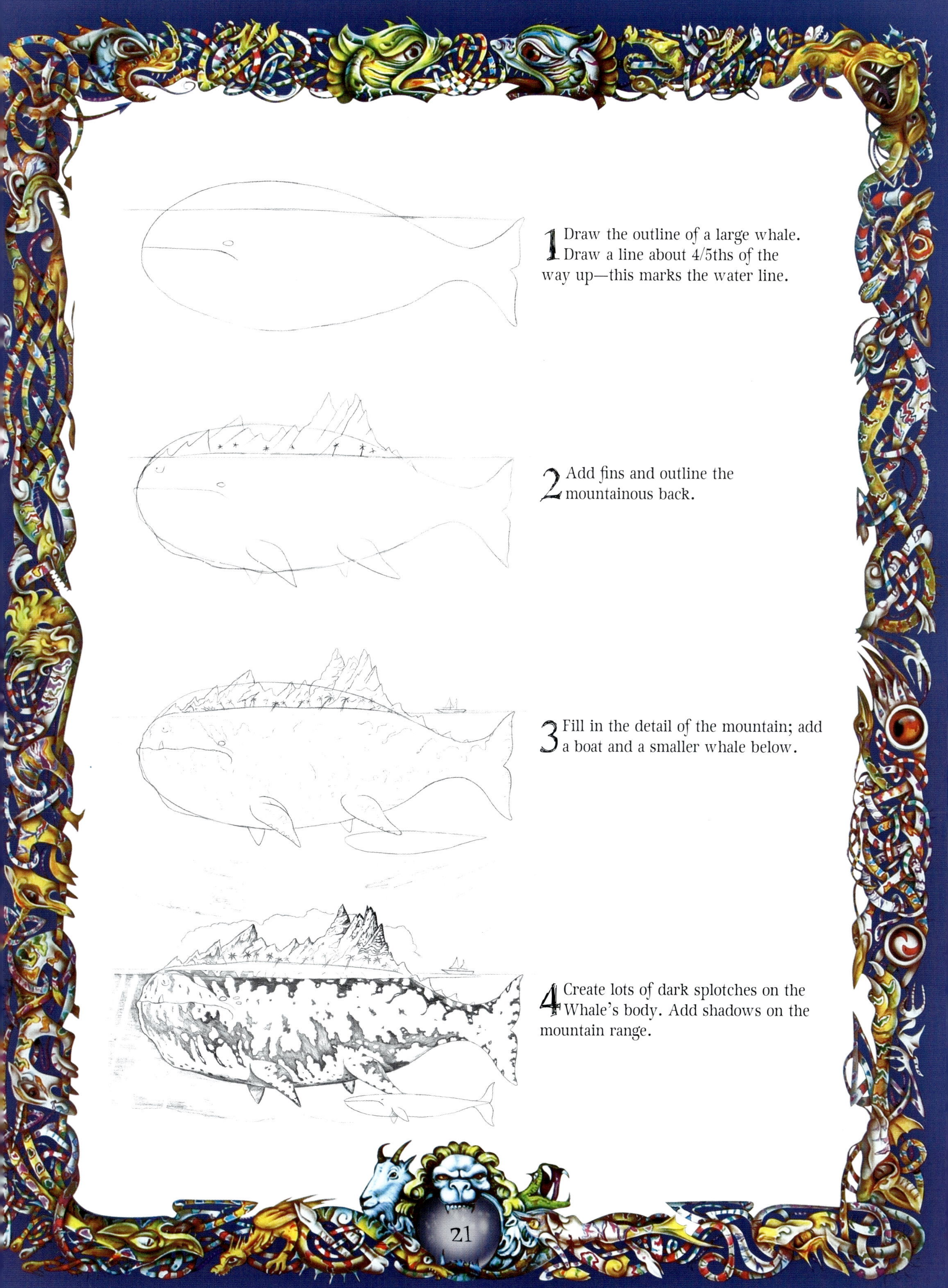

1 Draw the outline of a large whale. Draw a line about 4/5ths of the way up—this marks the water line.

2 Add fins and outline the mountainous back.

3 Fill in the detail of the mountain; add a boat and a smaller whale below.

4 Create lots of dark splotches on the Whale's body. Add shadows on the mountain range.

MERMAID

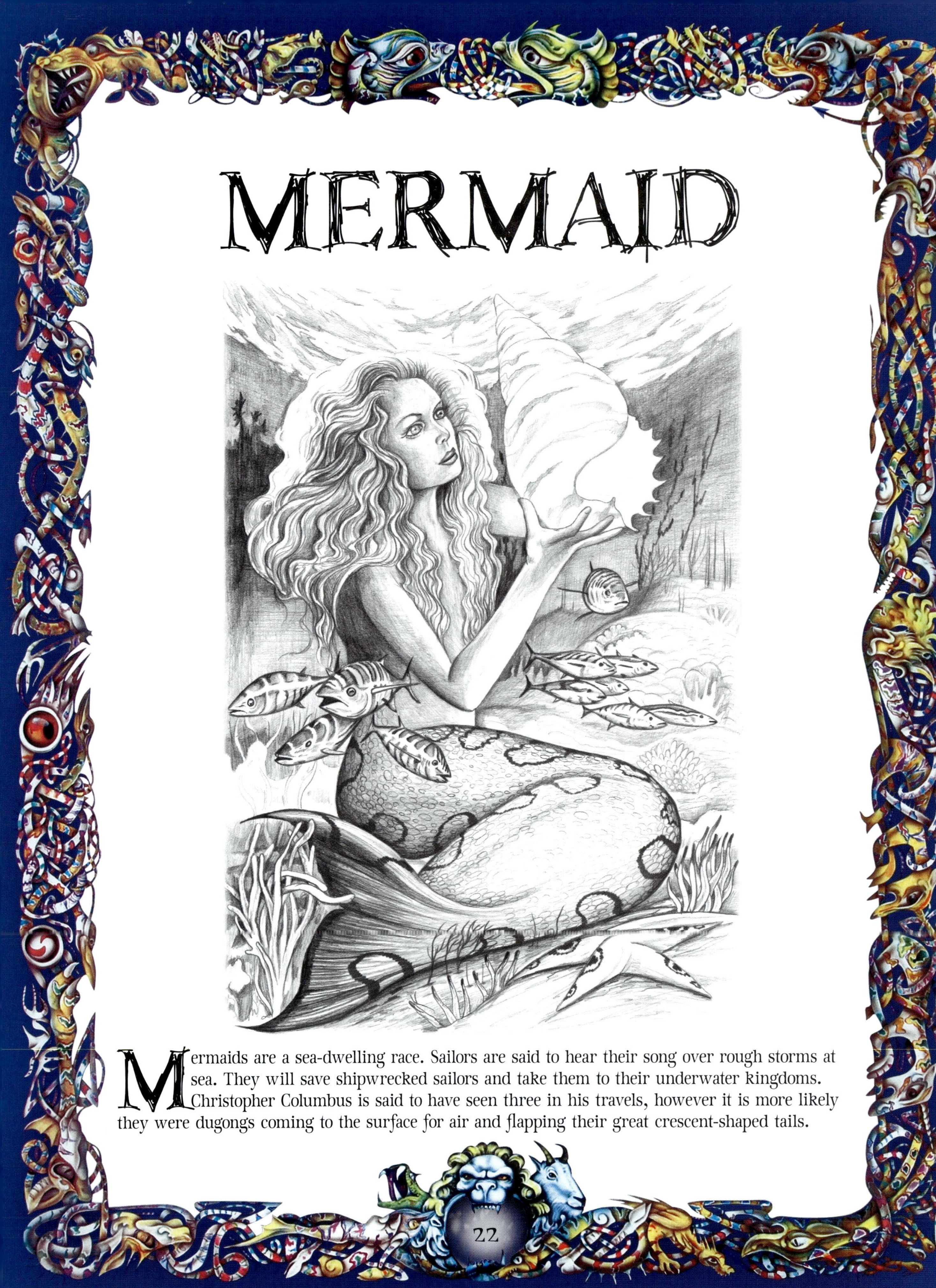

Mermaids are a sea-dwelling race. Sailors are said to hear their song over rough storms at sea. They will save shipwrecked sailors and take them to their underwater kingdoms. Christopher Columbus is said to have seen three in his travels, however it is more likely they were dugongs coming to the surface for air and flapping their great crescent-shaped tails.

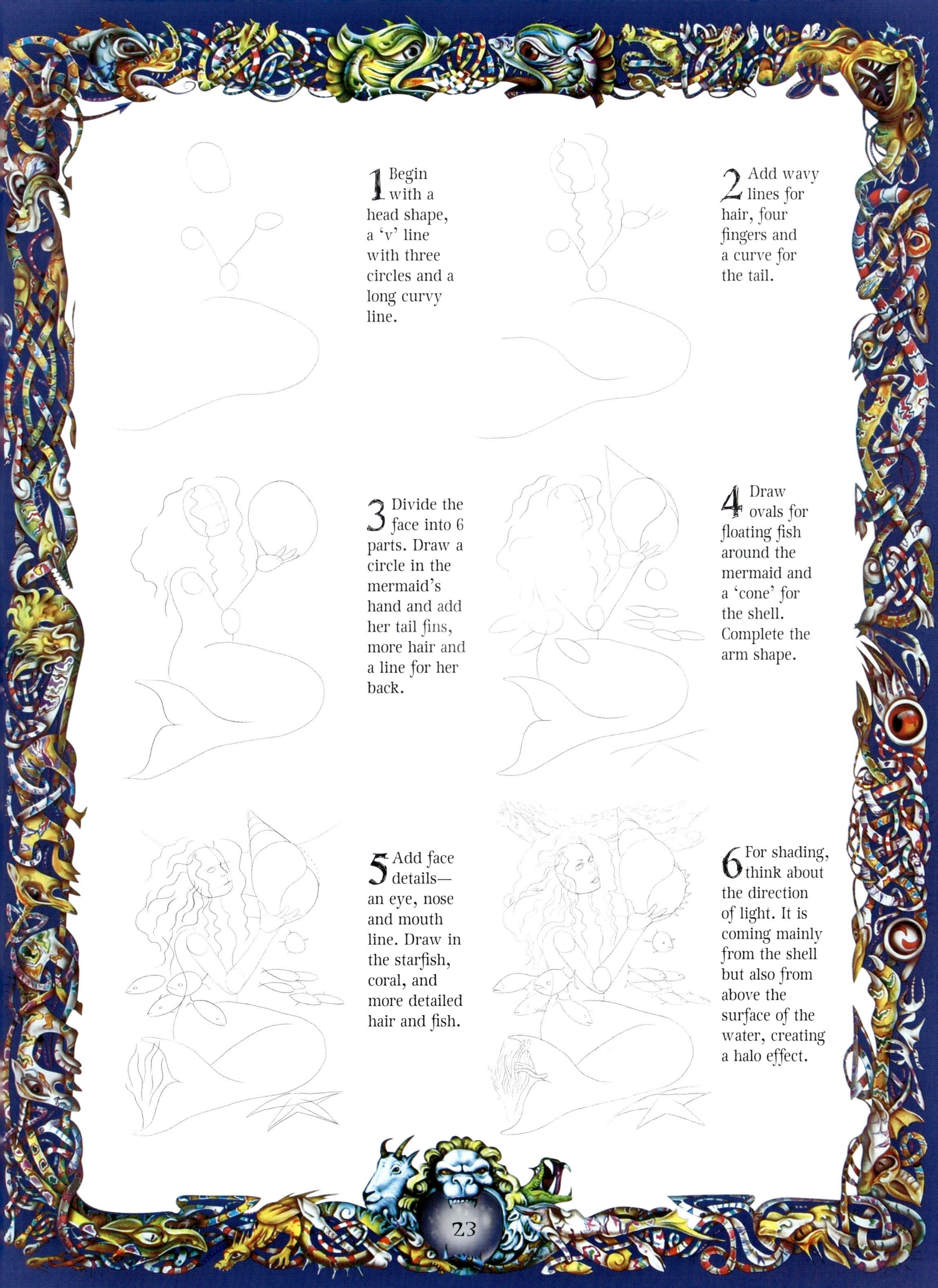

1 Begin with a head shape, a 'v' line with three circles and a long curvy line.

2 Add wavy lines for hair, four fingers and a curve for the tail.

3 Divide the face into 6 parts. Draw a circle in the mermaid's hand and add her tail fins, more hair and a line for her back.

4 Draw ovals for floating fish around the mermaid and a 'cone' for the shell. Complete the arm shape.

5 Add face details—an eye, nose and mouth line. Draw in the starfish, coral, and more detailed hair and fish.

6 For shading, think about the direction of light. It is coming mainly from the shell but also from above the surface of the water, creating a halo effect.

SPHINX

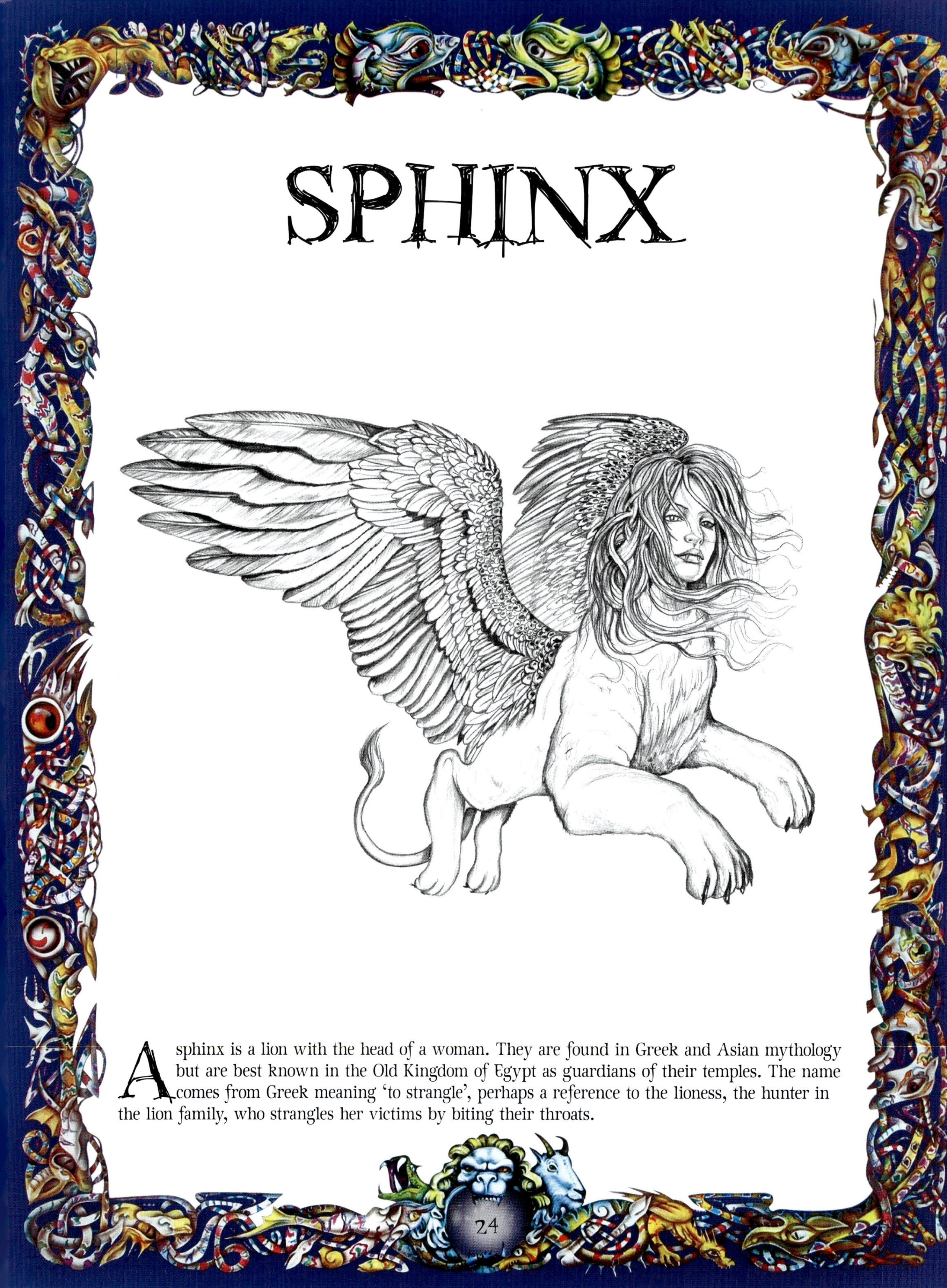

A sphinx is a lion with the head of a woman. They are found in Greek and Asian mythology but are best known in the Old Kingdom of Egypt as guardians of their temples. The name comes from Greek meaning ‘to strangle’, perhaps a reference to the lioness, the hunter in the lion family, who strangles her victims by biting their throats.

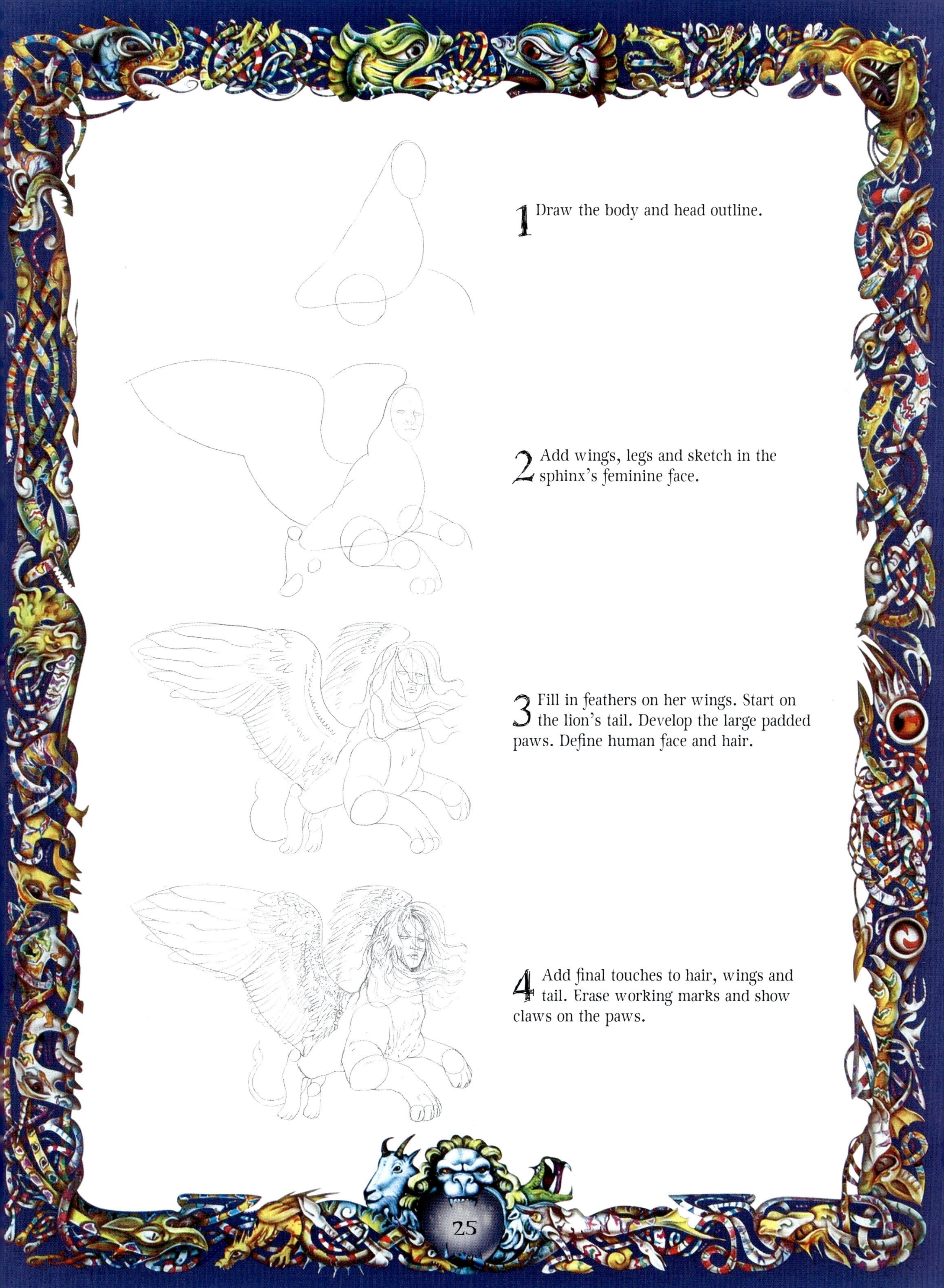

1 Draw the body and head outline.

2 Add wings, legs and sketch in the sphinx's feminine face.

3 Fill in feathers on her wings. Start on the lion's tail. Develop the large padded paws. Define human face and hair.

4 Add final touches to hair, wings and tail. Erase working marks and show claws on the paws.

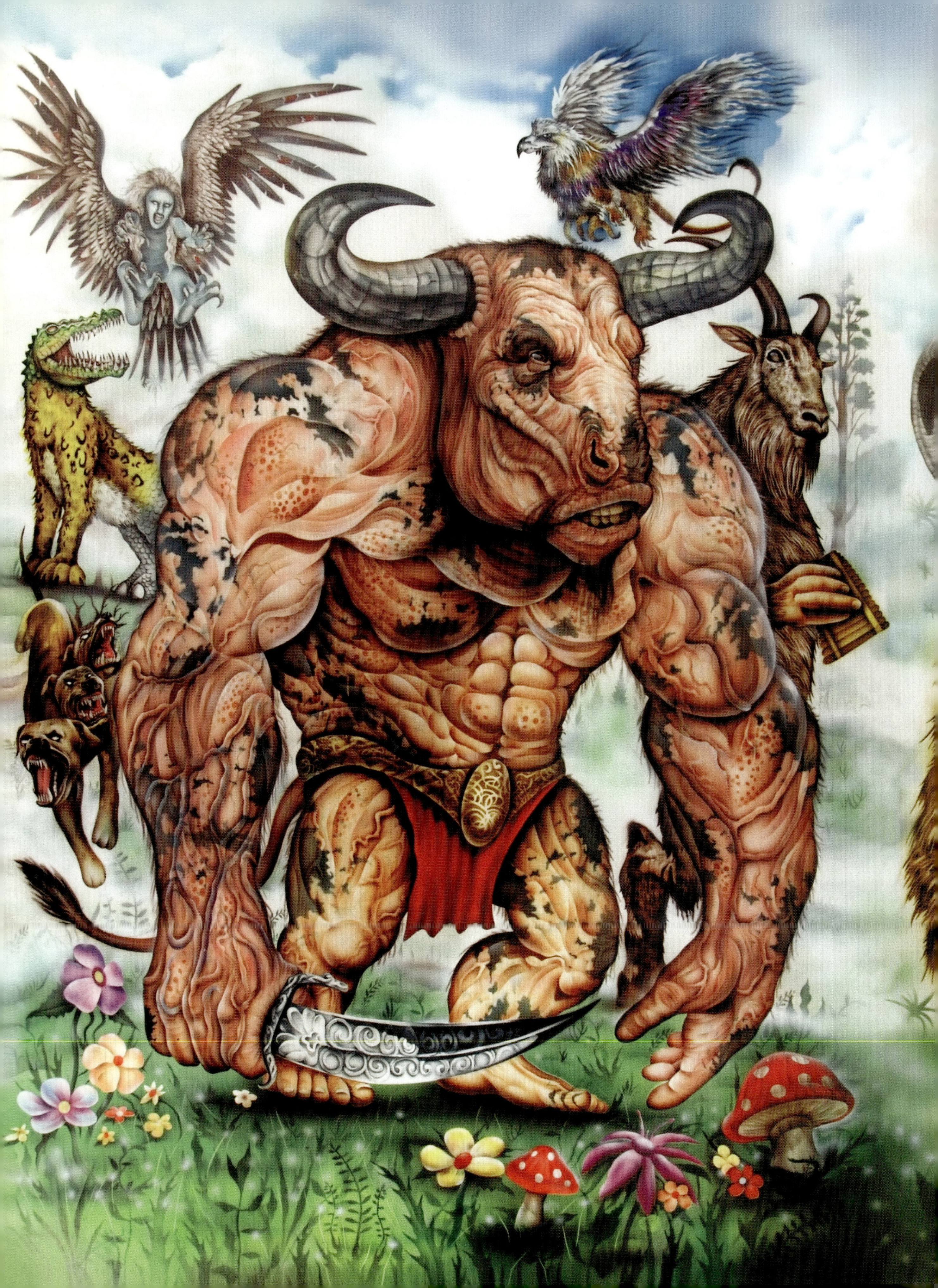

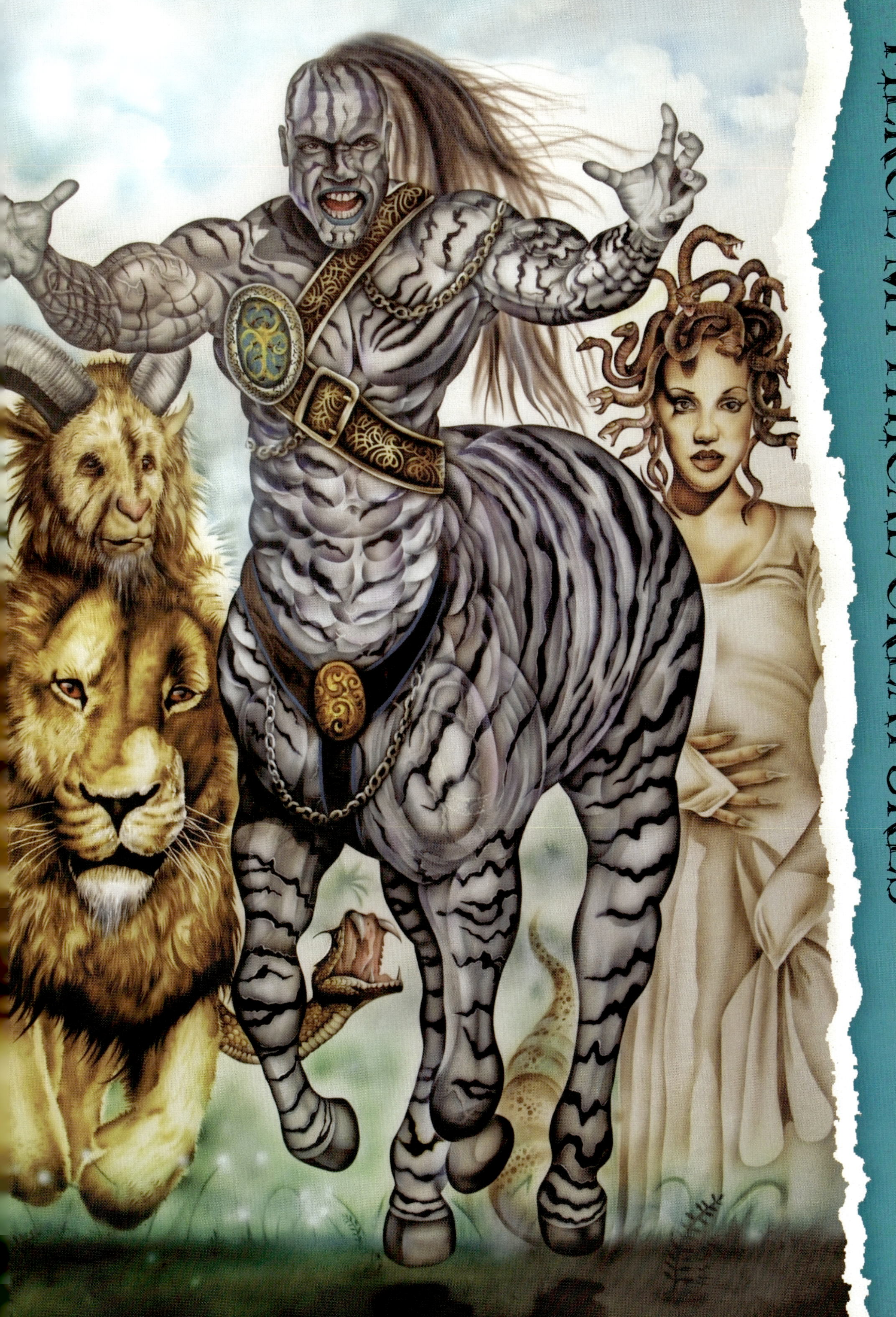

FIERCE MYTHICAL CREATURES

MINOTAUR

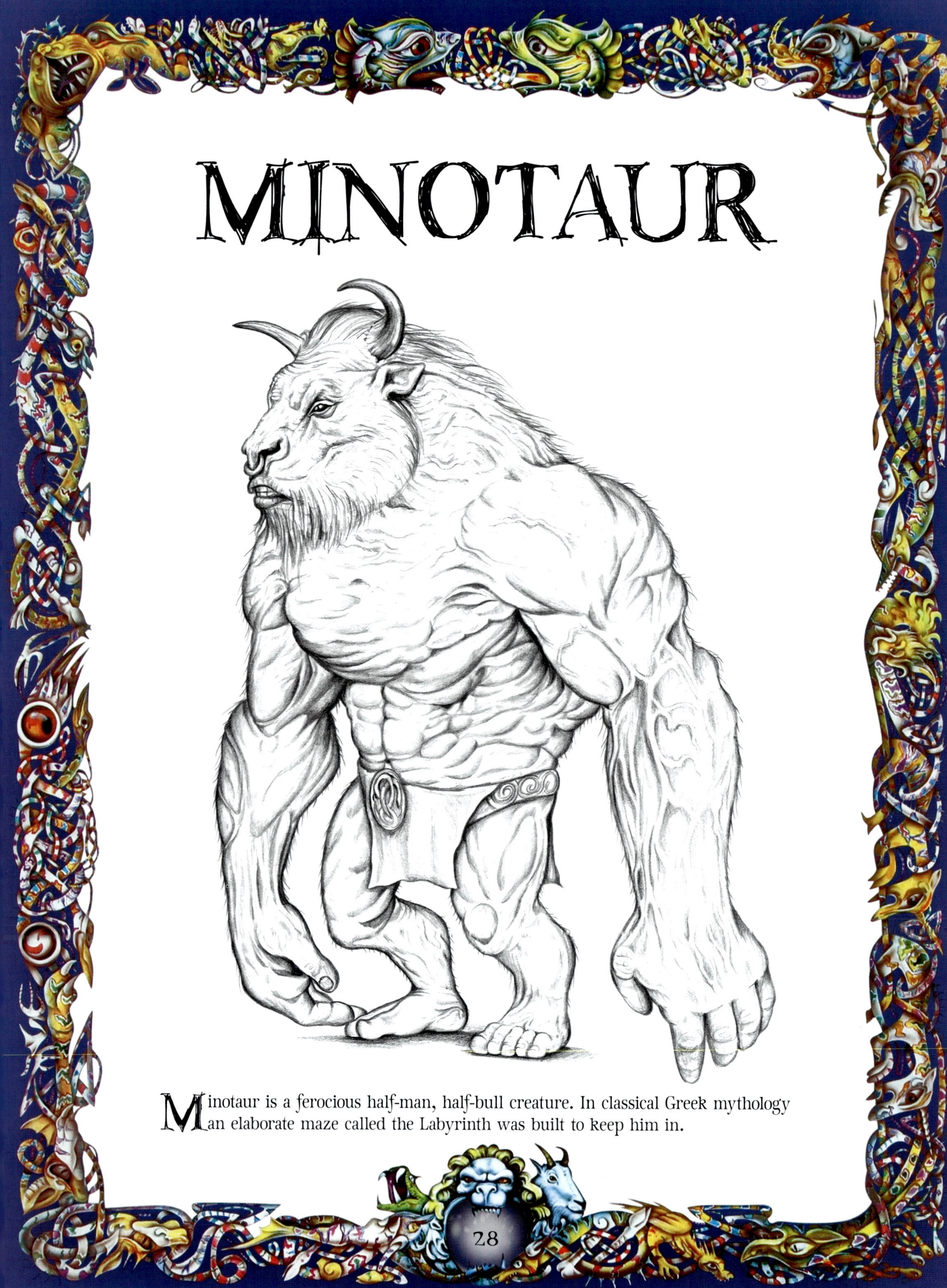

Minotaur is a ferocious half-man, half-bull creature. In classical Greek mythology an elaborate maze called the Labyrinth was built to keep him in.

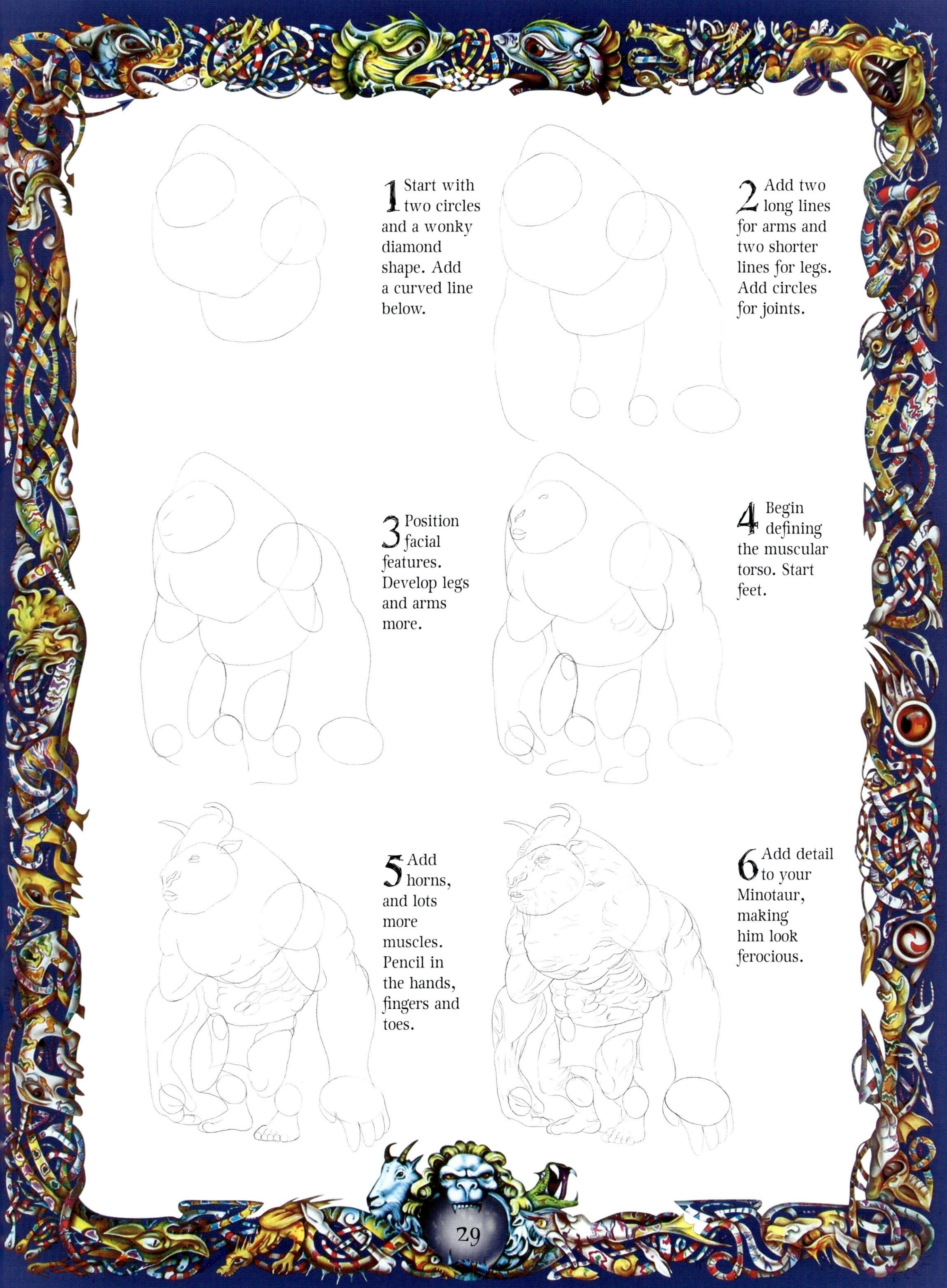

1 Start with two circles and a wonky diamond shape. Add a curved line below.

2 Add two long lines for arms and two shorter lines for legs. Add circles for joints.

3 Position facial features. Develop legs and arms more.

4 Begin defining the muscular torso. Start feet.

5 Add horns, and lots more muscles. Pencil in the hands, fingers and toes.

6 Add detail to your Minotaur, making him look ferocious.

SATYR

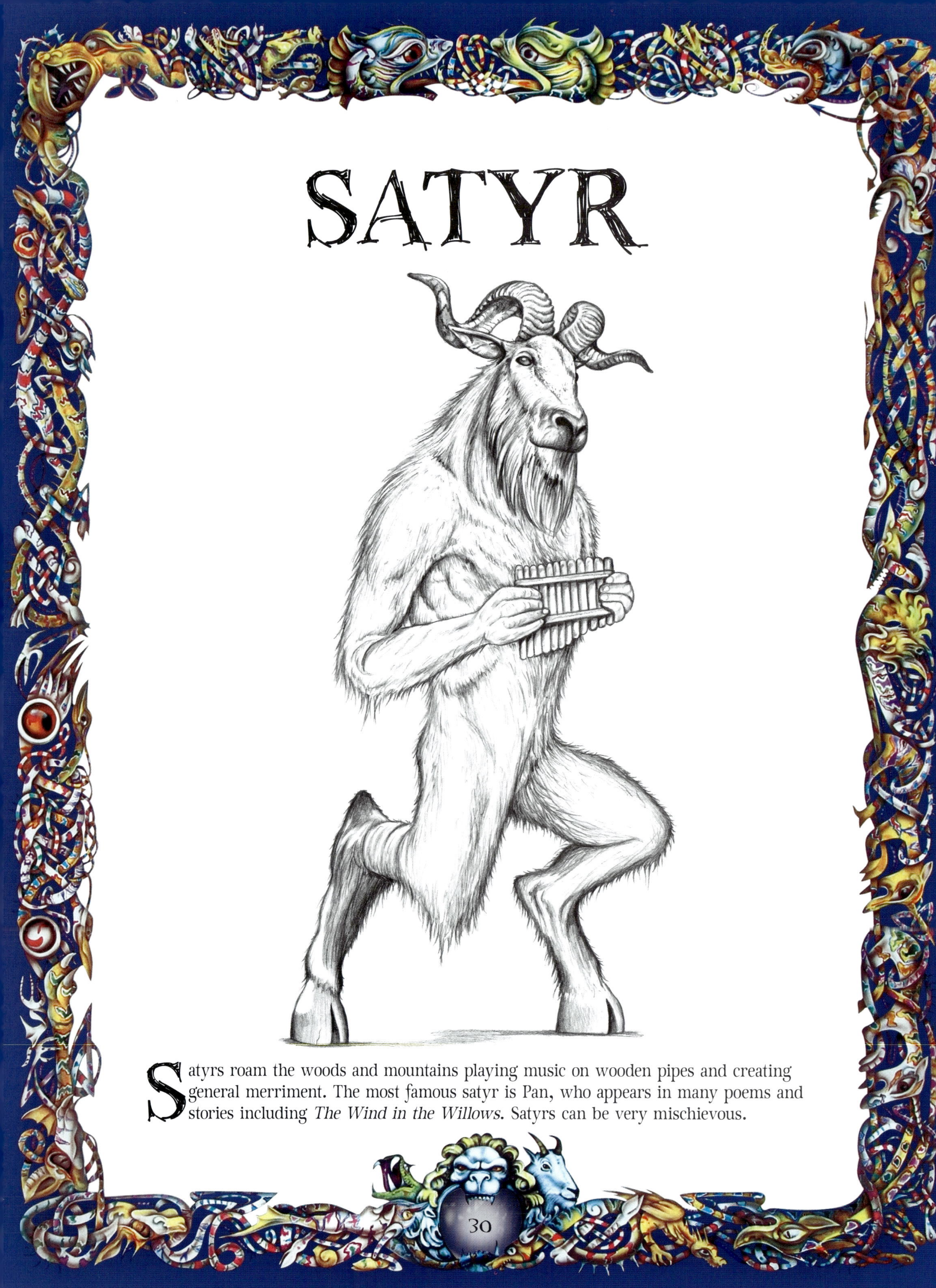

Satyrs roam the woods and mountains playing music on wooden pipes and creating general merriment. The most famous satyr is Pan, who appears in many poems and stories including *The Wind in the Willows*. Satyrs can be very mischievous.

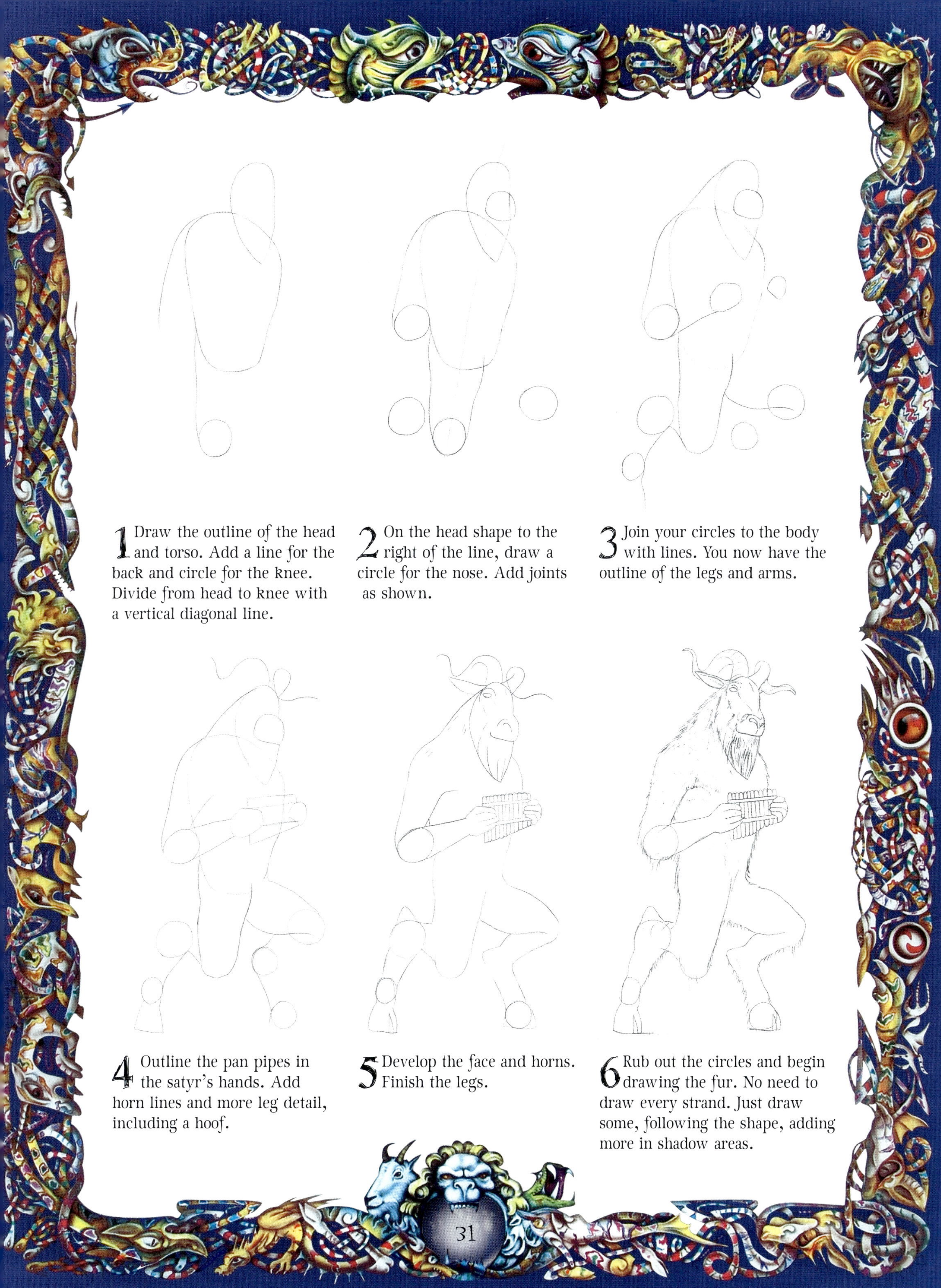

1 Draw the outline of the head and torso. Add a line for the back and circle for the knee. Divide from head to knee with a vertical diagonal line.

2 On the head shape to the right of the line, draw a circle for the nose. Add joints as shown.

3 Join your circles to the body with lines. You now have the outline of the legs and arms.

4 Outline the pan pipes in the satyr's hands. Add horn lines and more leg detail, including a hoof.

5 Develop the face and horns. Finish the legs.

6 Rub out the circles and begin drawing the fur. No need to draw every strand. Just draw some, following the shape, adding more in shadow areas.

GRIFFIN

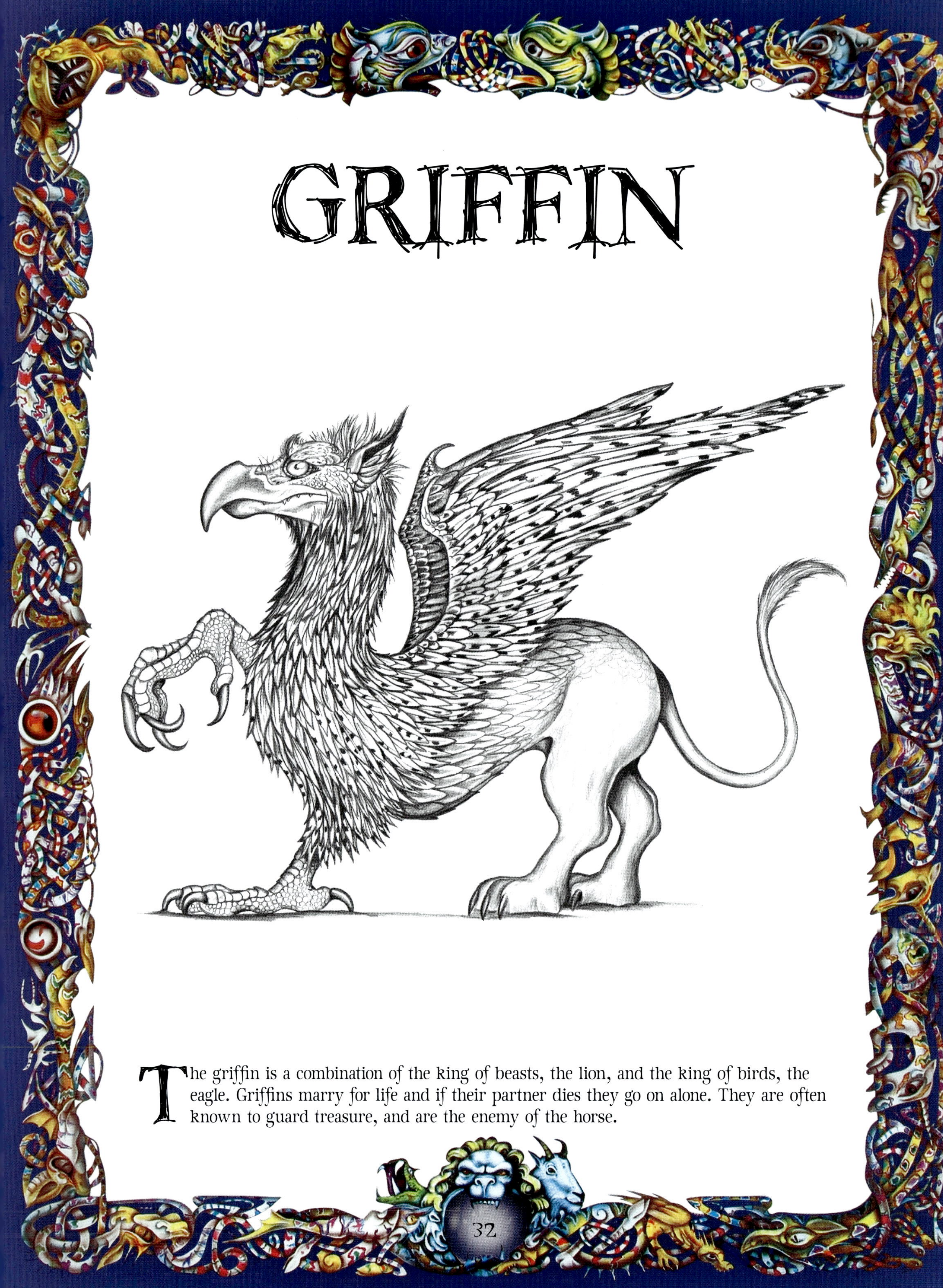

The griffin is a combination of the king of beasts, the lion, and the king of birds, the eagle. Griffins marry for life and if their partner dies they go on alone. They are often known to guard treasure, and are the enemy of the horse.

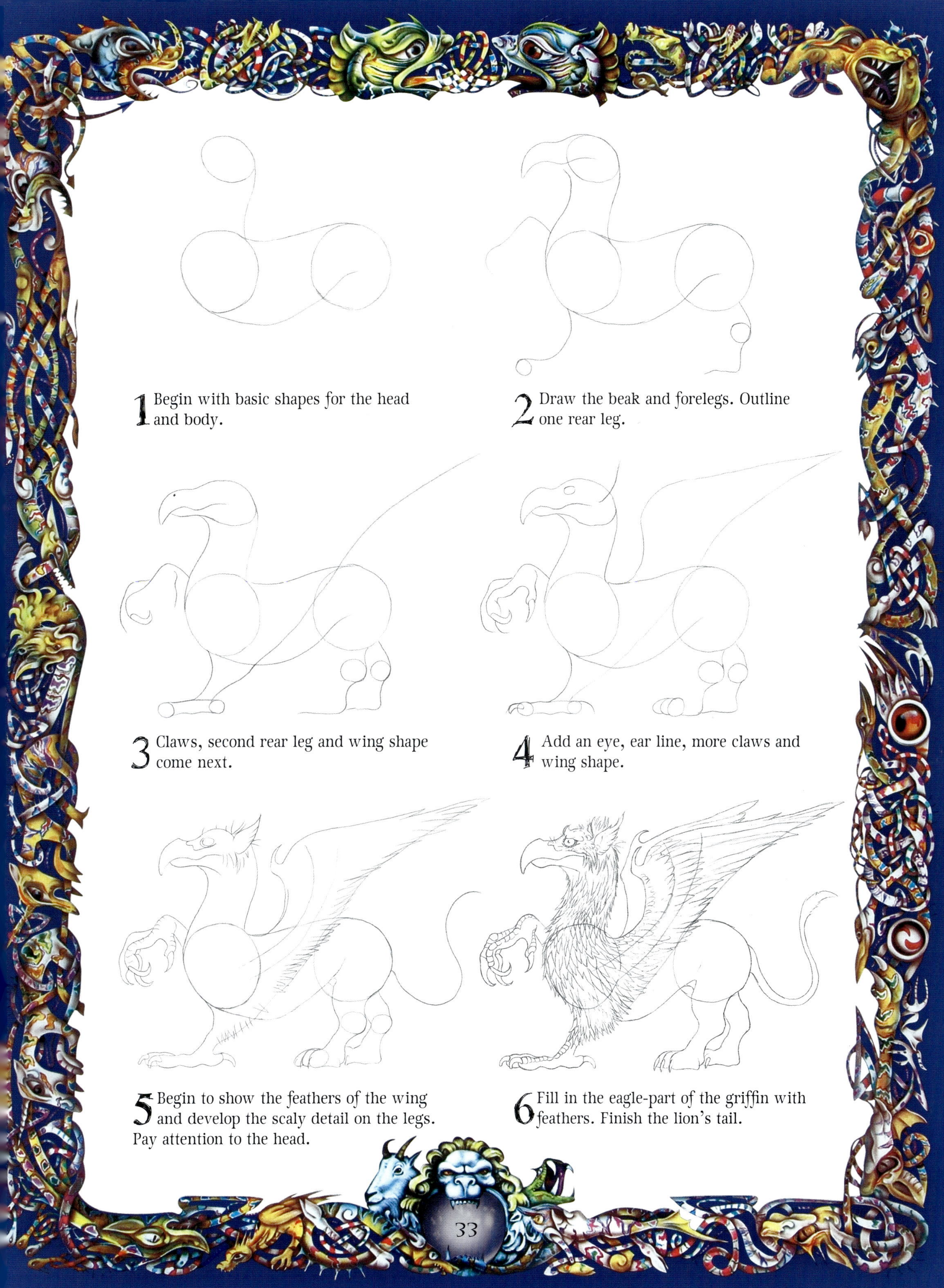

1 Begin with basic shapes for the head and body.

2 Draw the beak and forelegs. Outline one rear leg.

3 Claws, second rear leg and wing shape come next.

4 Add an eye, ear line, more claws and wing shape.

5 Begin to show the feathers of the wing and develop the scaly detail on the legs. Pay attention to the head.

6 Fill in the eagle-part of the griffin with feathers. Finish the lion's tail.

GORGON

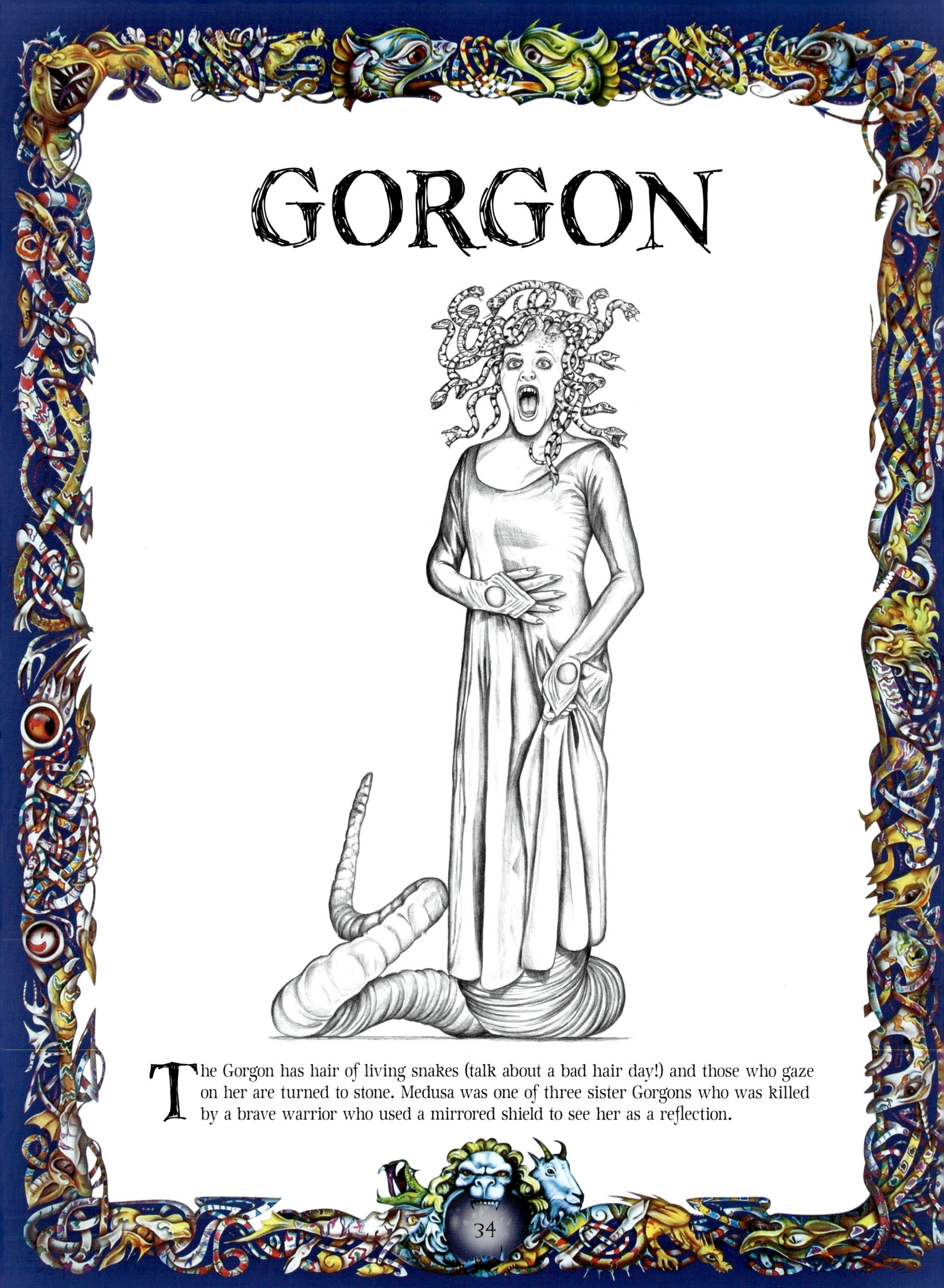

The Gorgon has hair of living snakes (talk about a bad hair day!) and those who gaze on her are turned to stone. Medusa was one of three sister Gorgons who was killed by a brave warrior who used a mirrored shield to see her as a reflection.

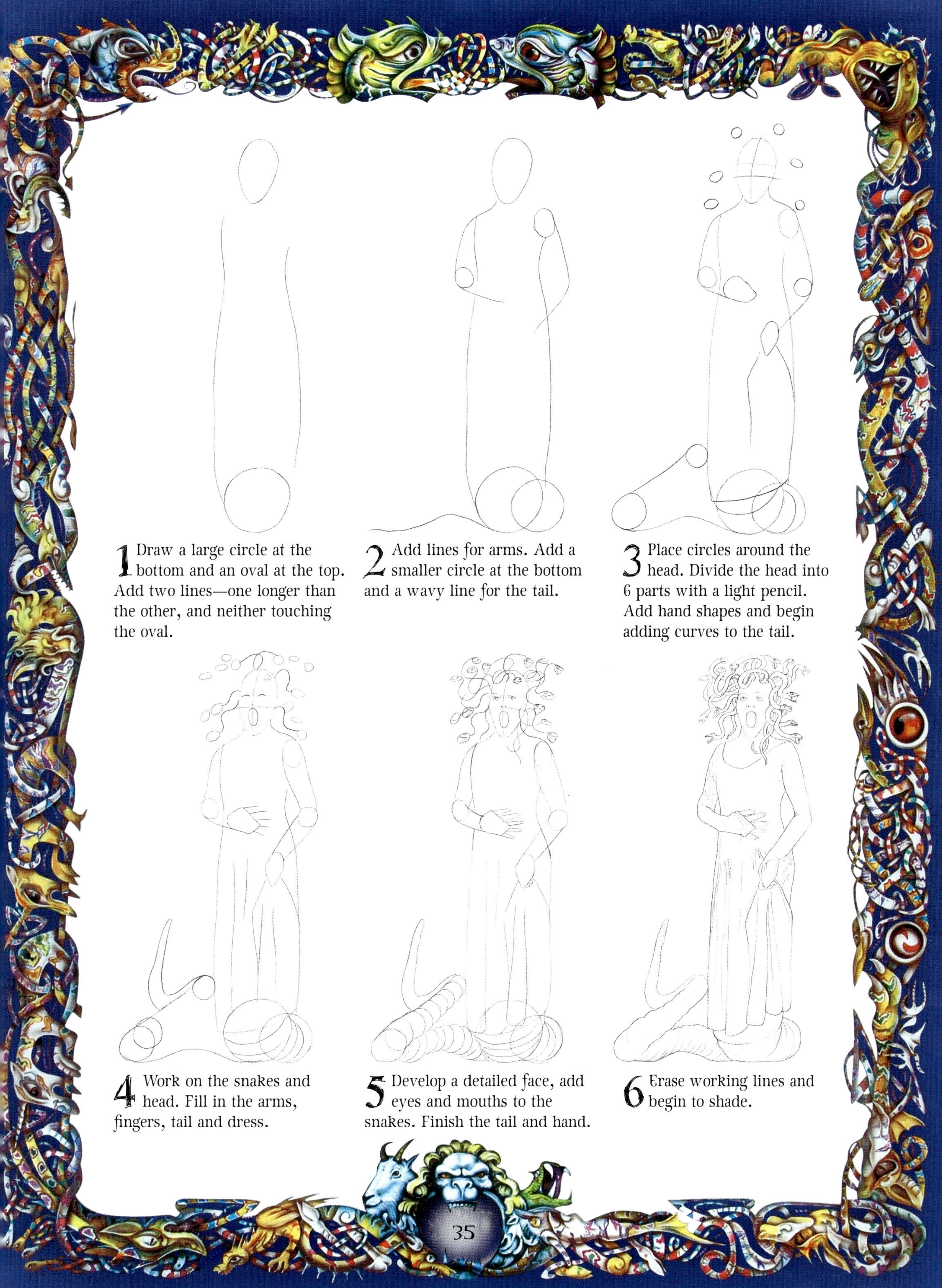

1 Draw a large circle at the bottom and an oval at the top. Add two lines—one longer than the other, and neither touching the oval.

2 Add lines for arms. Add a smaller circle at the bottom and a wavy line for the tail.

3 Place circles around the head. Divide the head into 6 parts with a light pencil. Add hand shapes and begin adding curves to the tail.

4 Work on the snakes and head. Fill in the arms, fingers, tail and dress.

5 Develop a detailed face, add eyes and mouths to the snakes. Finish the tail and hand.

6 Erase working lines and begin to shade.

CHIMERA

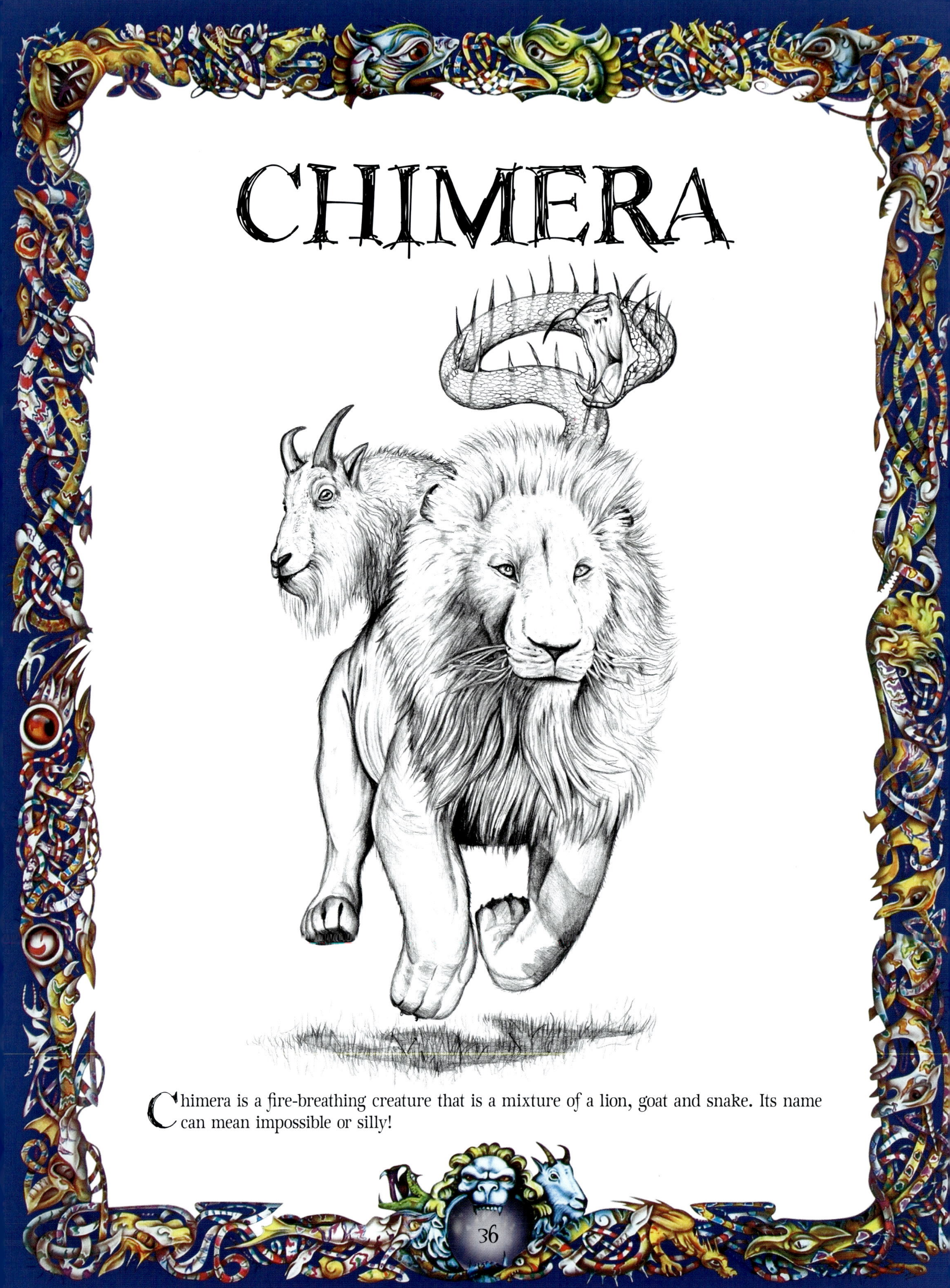

Chimera is a fire-breathing creature that is a mixture of a lion, goat and snake. Its name can mean impossible or silly!

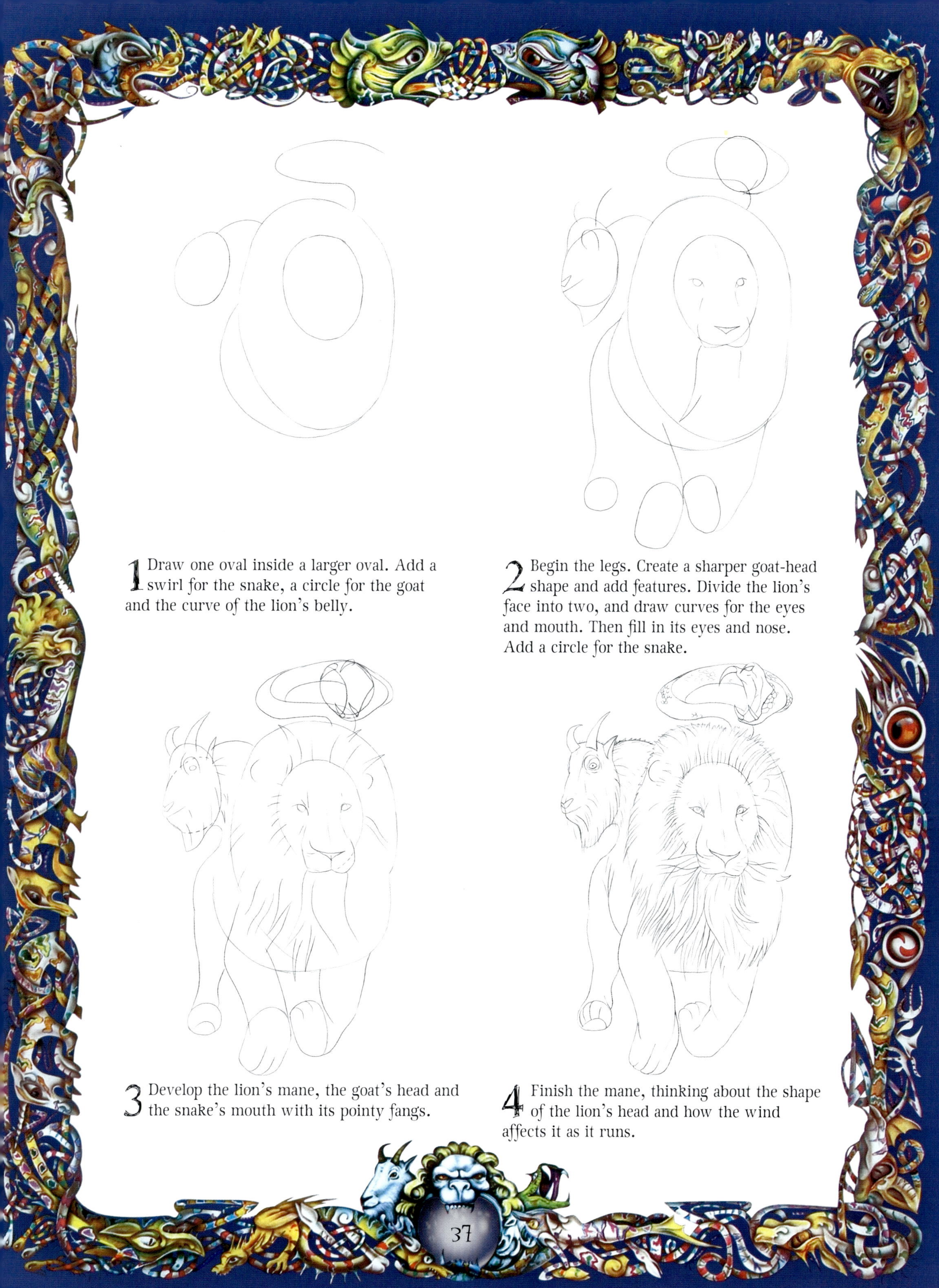

1 Draw one oval inside a larger oval. Add a swirl for the snake, a circle for the goat and the curve of the lion's belly.

2 Begin the legs. Create a sharper goat-head shape and add features. Divide the lion's face into two, and draw curves for the eyes and mouth. Then fill in its eyes and nose. Add a circle for the snake.

3 Develop the lion's mane, the goat's head and the snake's mouth with its pointy fangs.

4 Finish the mane, thinking about the shape of the lion's head and how the wind affects it as it runs.

CERBERUS

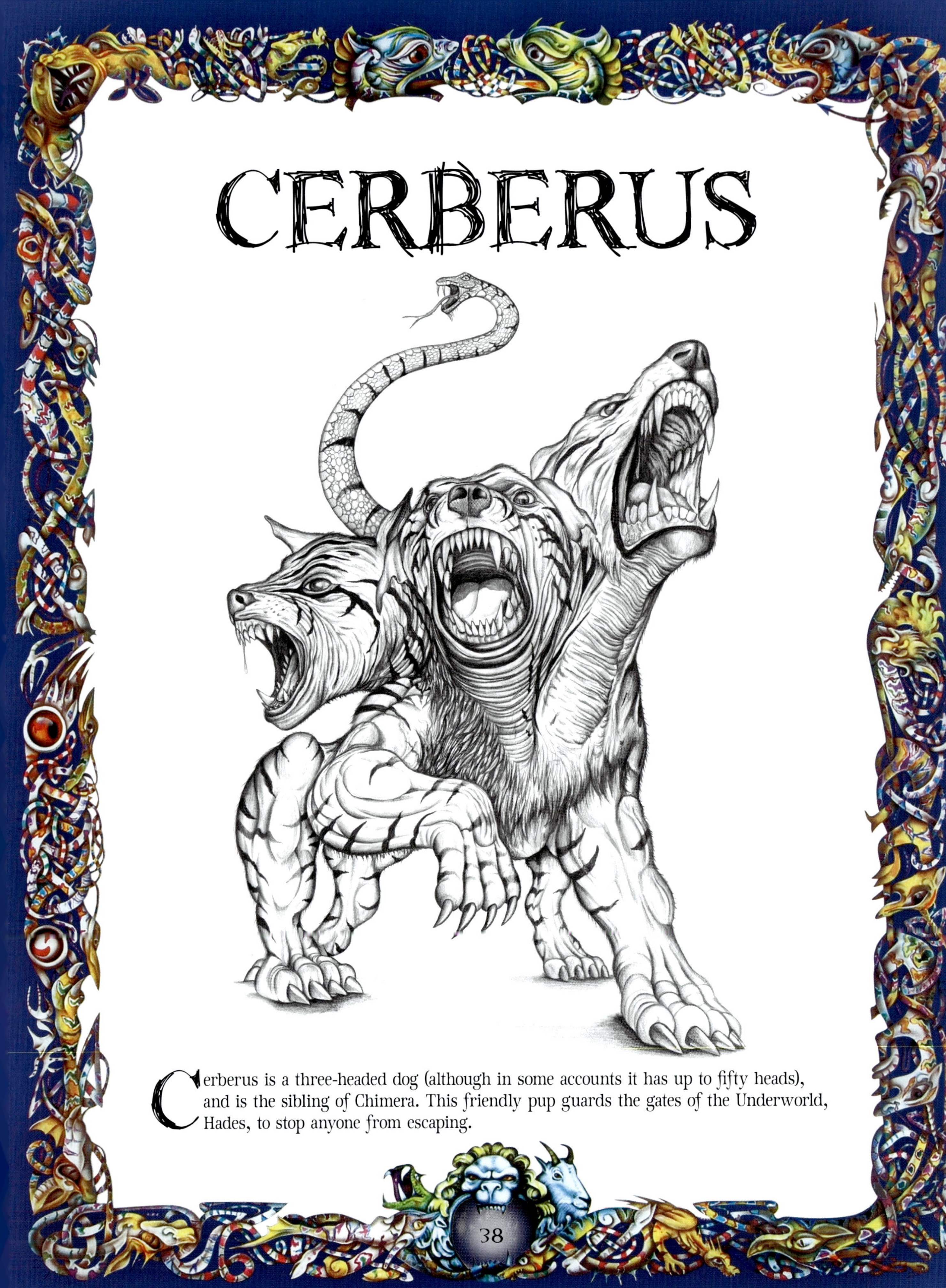

Cerberus is a three-headed dog (although in some accounts it has up to fifty heads), and is the sibling of Chimera. This friendly pup guards the gates of the Underworld, Hades, to stop anyone from escaping.

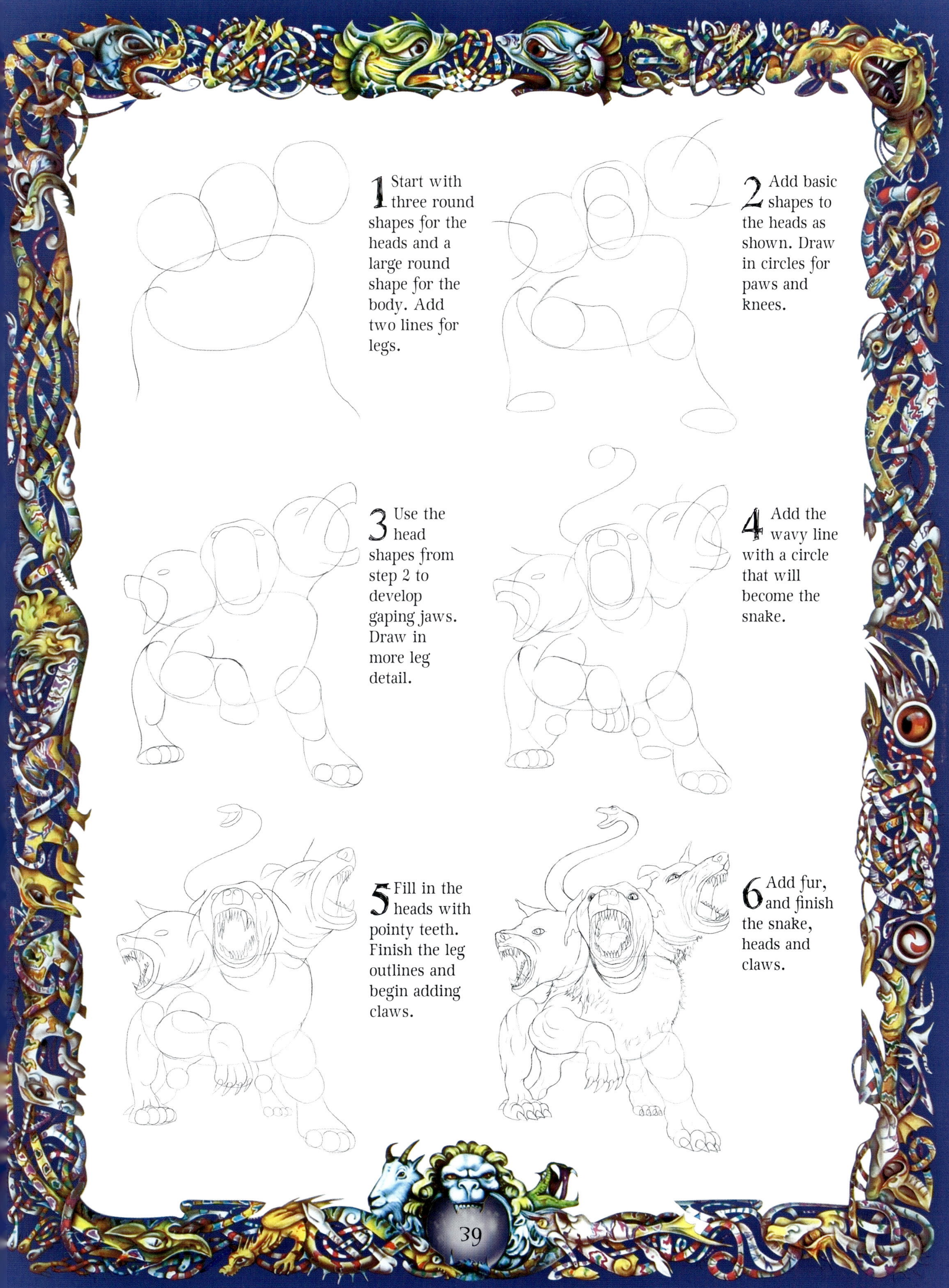

1 Start with three round shapes for the heads and a large round shape for the body. Add two lines for legs.

2 Add basic shapes to the heads as shown. Draw in circles for paws and knees.

3 Use the head shapes from step 2 to develop gaping jaws. Draw in more leg detail.

4 Add the wavy line with a circle that will become the snake.

5 Fill in the heads with pointy teeth. Finish the leg outlines and begin adding claws.

6 Add fur, and finish the snake, heads and claws.

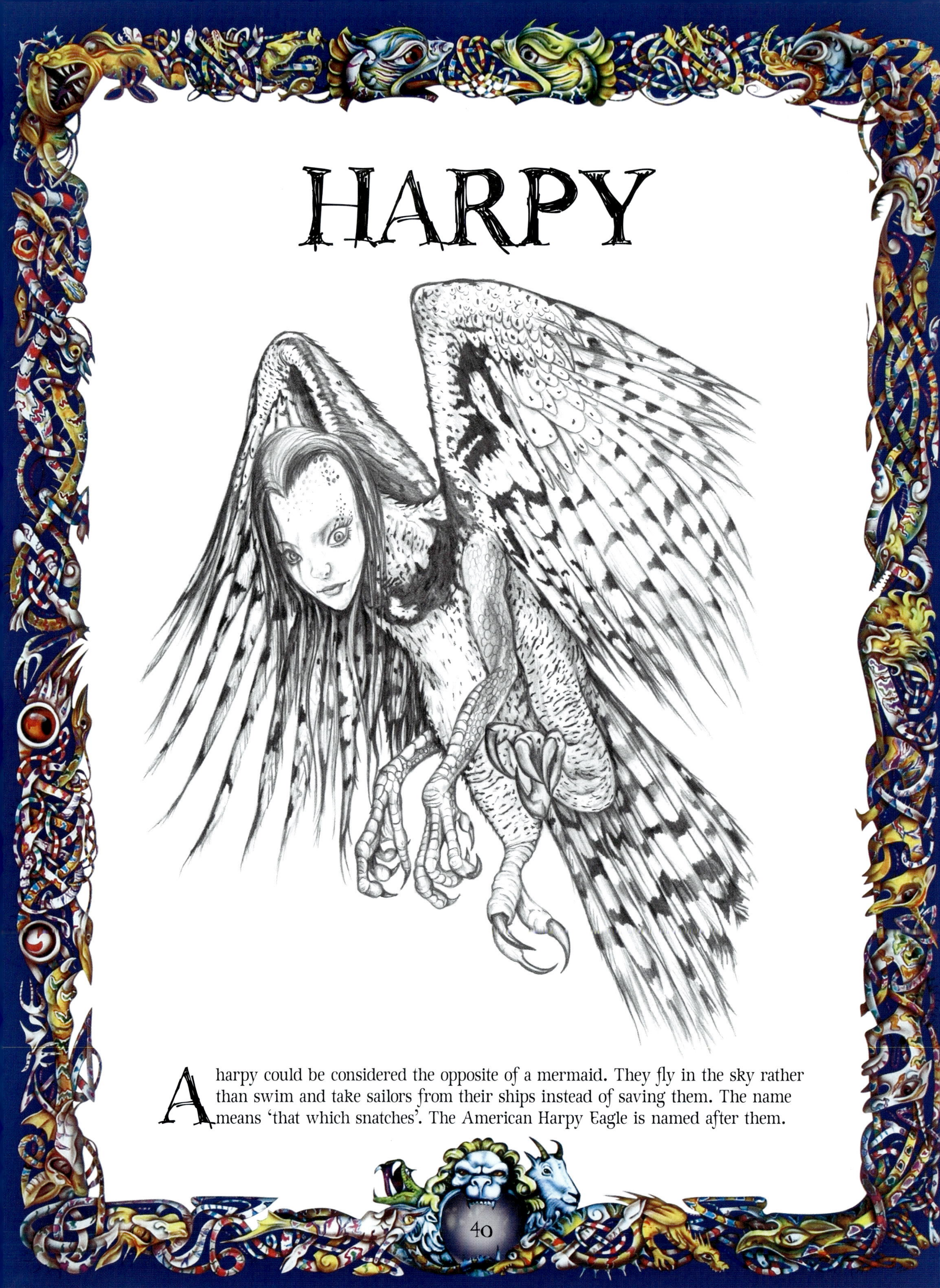

HARPY

A harpy could be considered the opposite of a mermaid. They fly in the sky rather than swim and take sailors from their ships instead of saving them. The name means 'that which snatches'. The American Harpy Eagle is named after them.

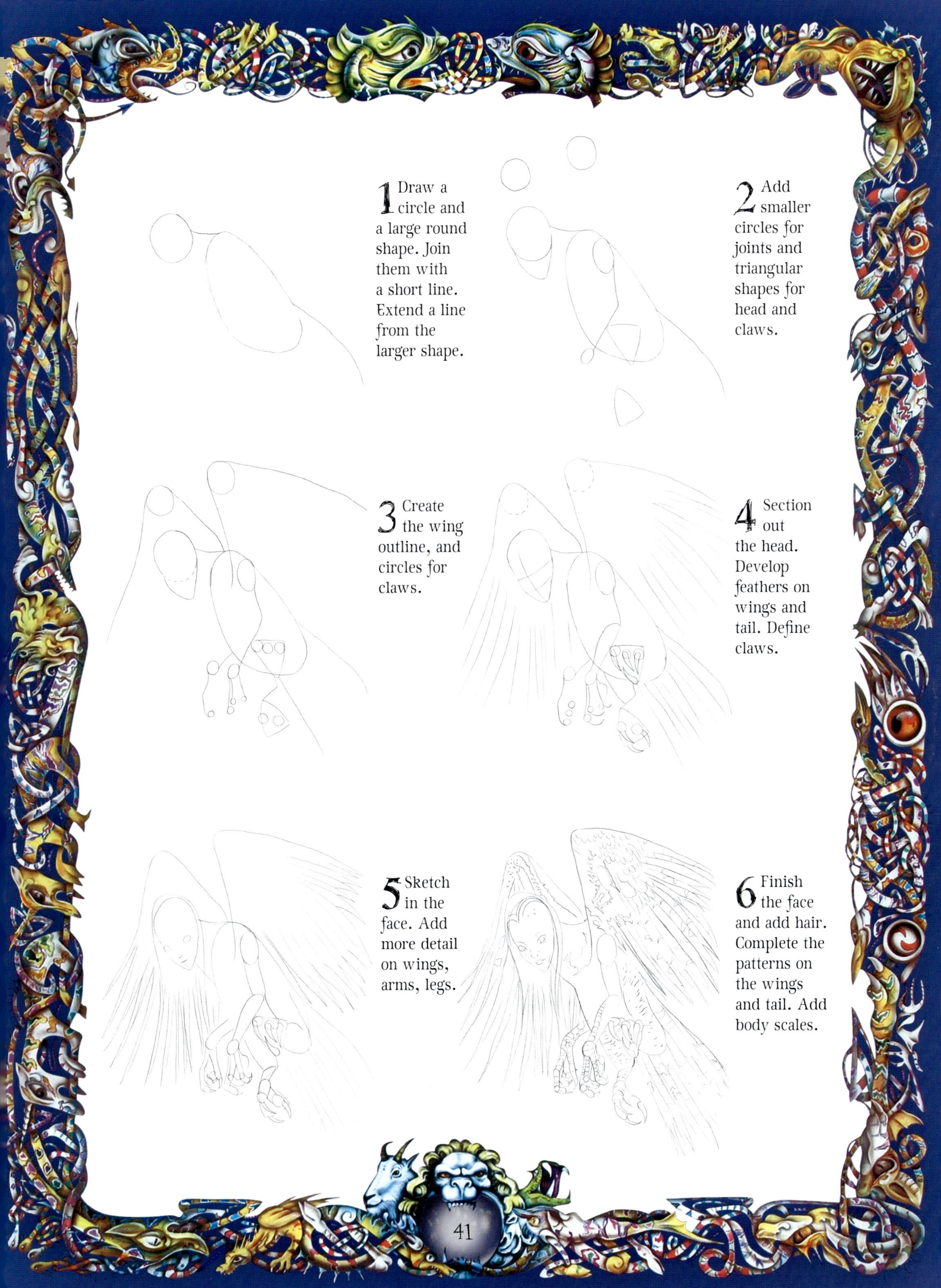

1 Draw a circle and a large round shape. Join them with a short line. Extend a line from the larger shape.

2 Add smaller circles for joints and triangular shapes for head and claws.

3 Create the wing outline, and circles for claws.

4 Section out the head. Develop feathers on wings and tail. Define claws.

5 Sketch in the face. Add more detail on wings, arms, legs.

6 Finish the face and add hair. Complete the patterns on the wings and tail. Add body scales.

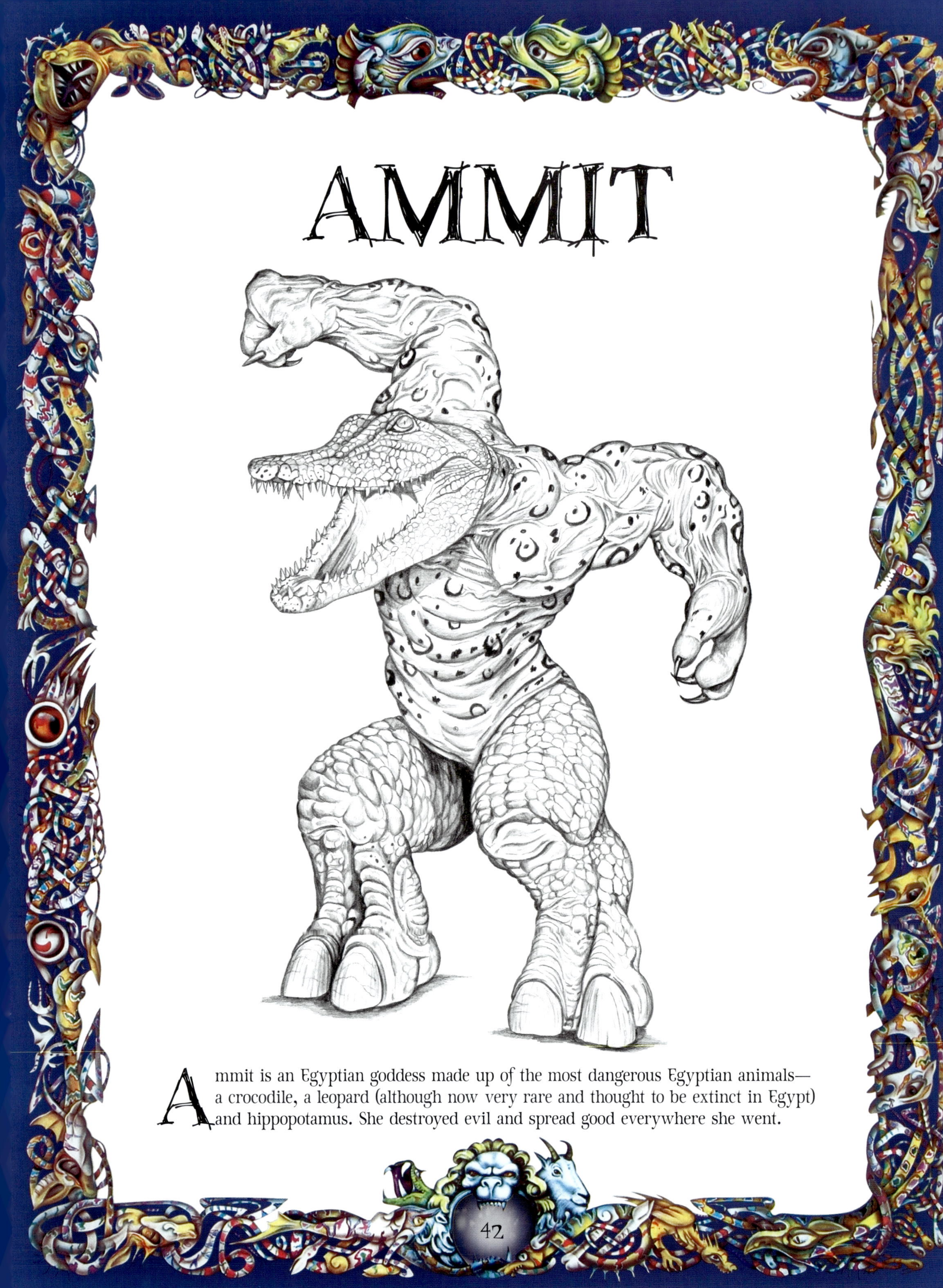

AMMIT

Ammit is an Egyptian goddess made up of the most dangerous Egyptian animals—a crocodile, a leopard (although now very rare and thought to be extinct in Egypt) and hippopotamus. She destroyed evil and spread good everywhere she went.

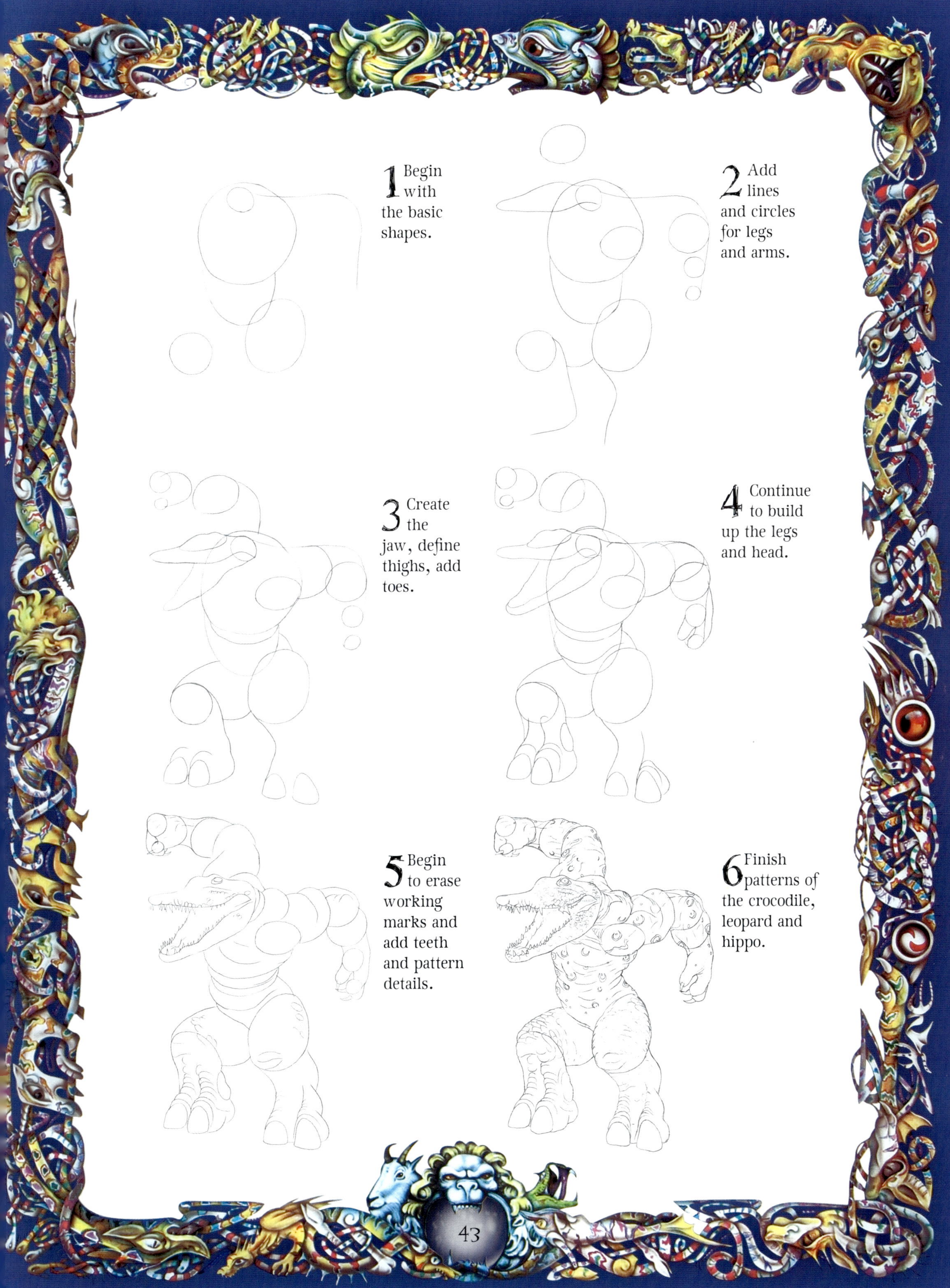

1 Begin with the basic shapes.

2 Add lines and circles for legs and arms.

3 Create the jaw, define thighs, add toes.

4 Continue to build up the legs and head.

5 Begin to erase working marks and add teeth and pattern details.

6 Finish patterns of the crocodile, leopard and hippo.

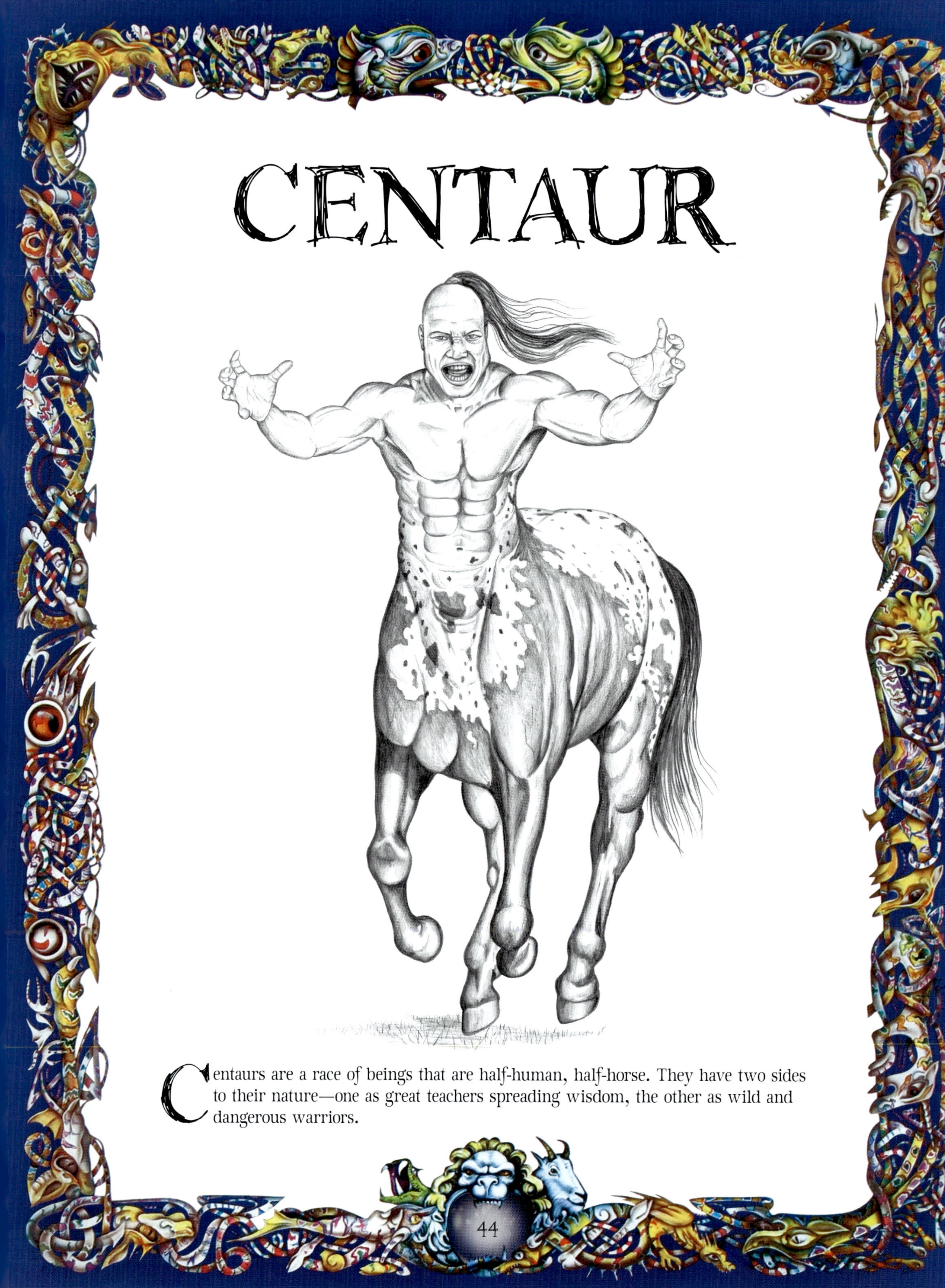

CENTAUR

Centaurs are a race of beings that are half-human, half-horse. They have two sides to their nature—one as great teachers spreading wisdom, the other as wild and dangerous warriors.

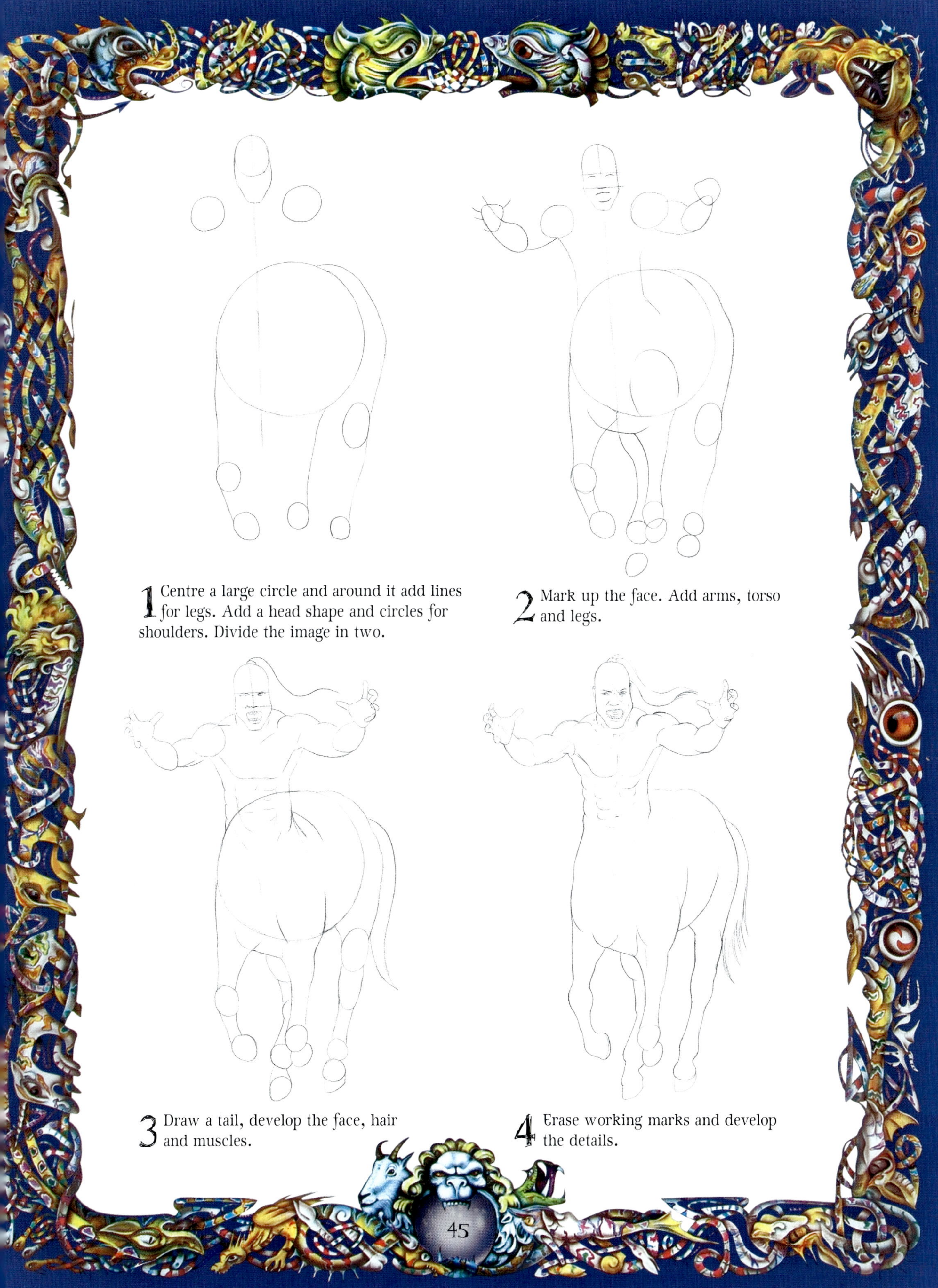

1 Centre a large circle and around it add lines for legs. Add a head shape and circles for shoulders. Divide the image in two.

2 Mark up the face. Add arms, torso and legs.

3 Draw a tail, develop the face, hair and muscles.

4 Erase working marks and develop the details.

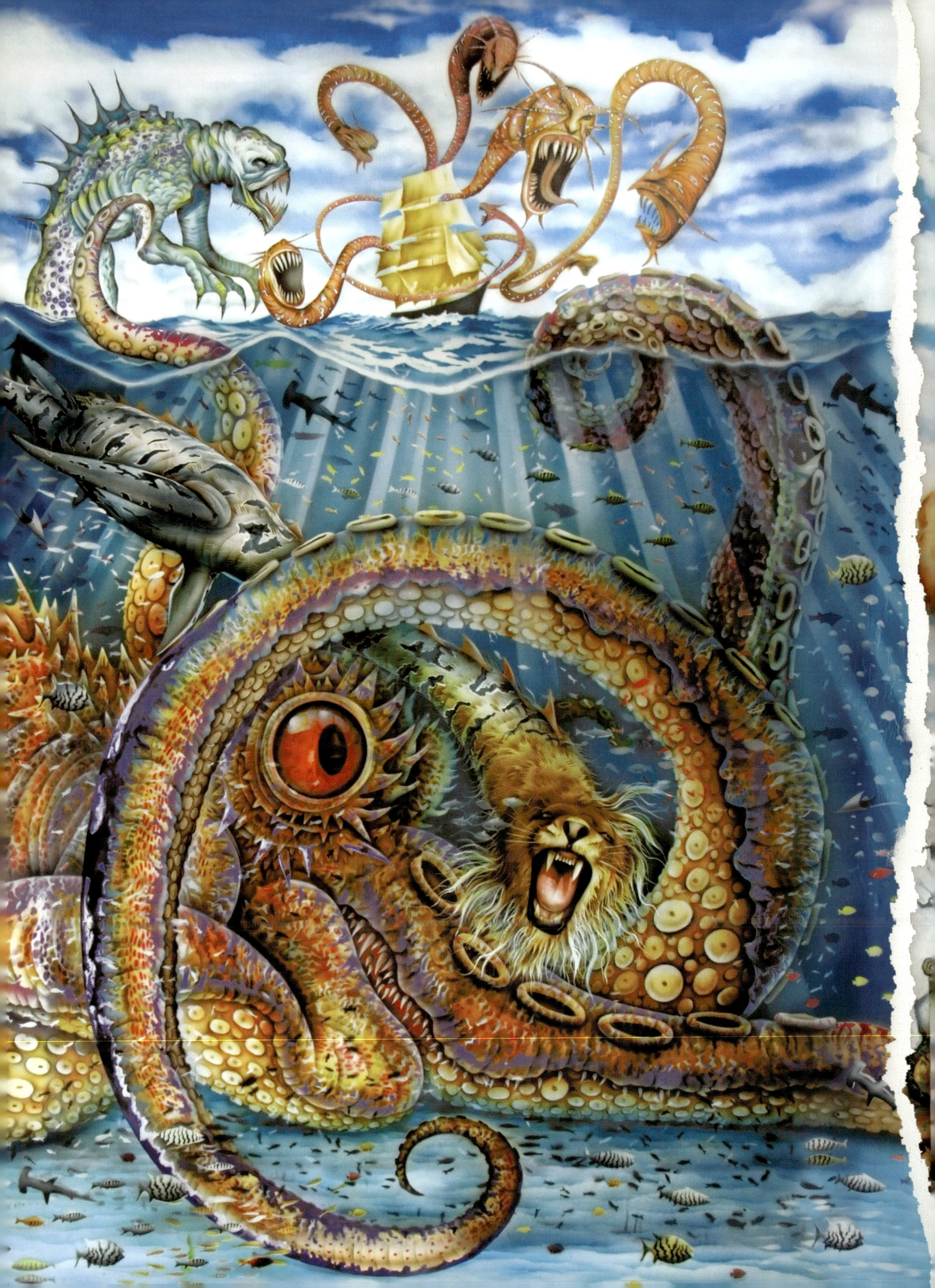

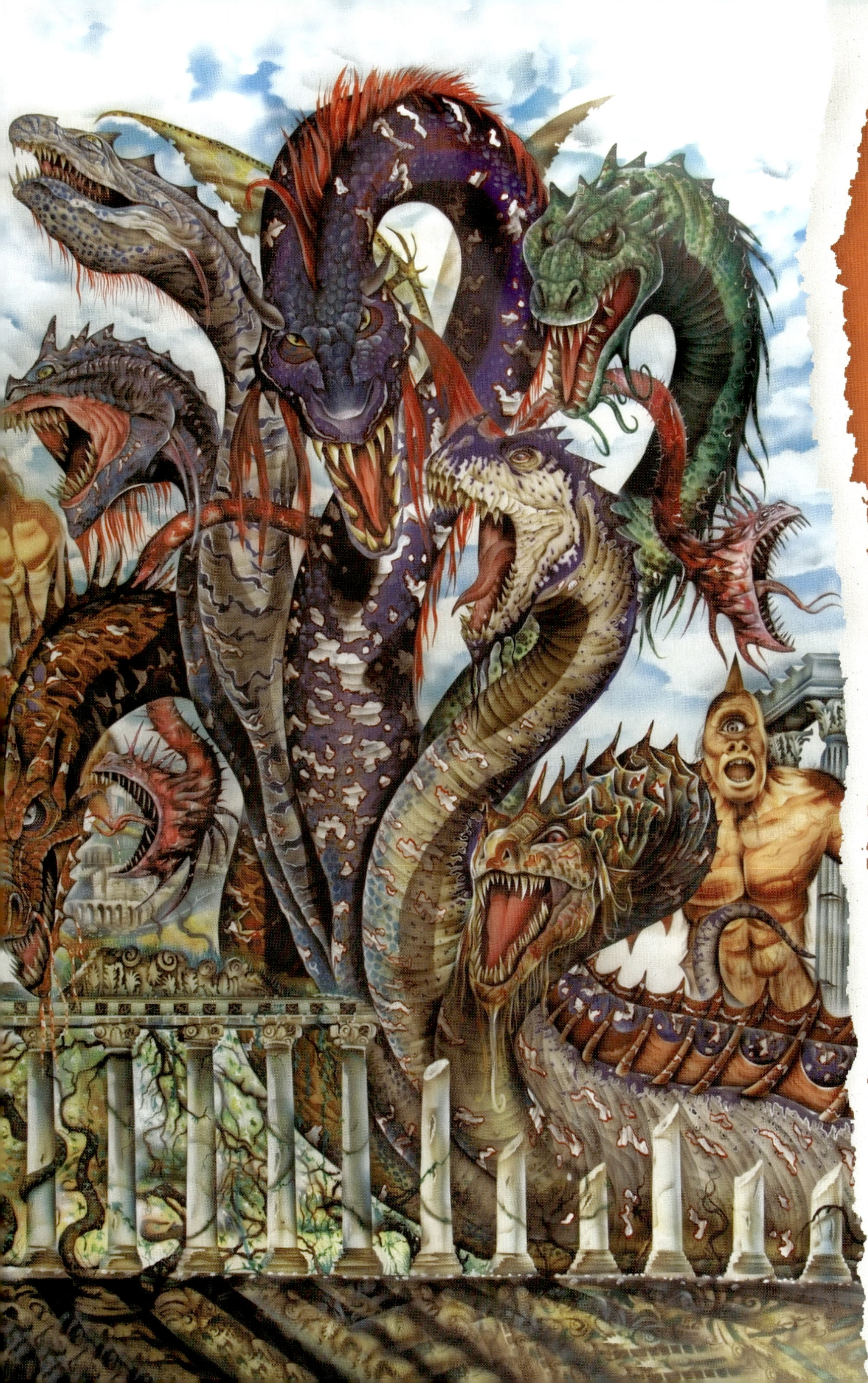

VERY DANGEROUS MYTHICAL CREATURES

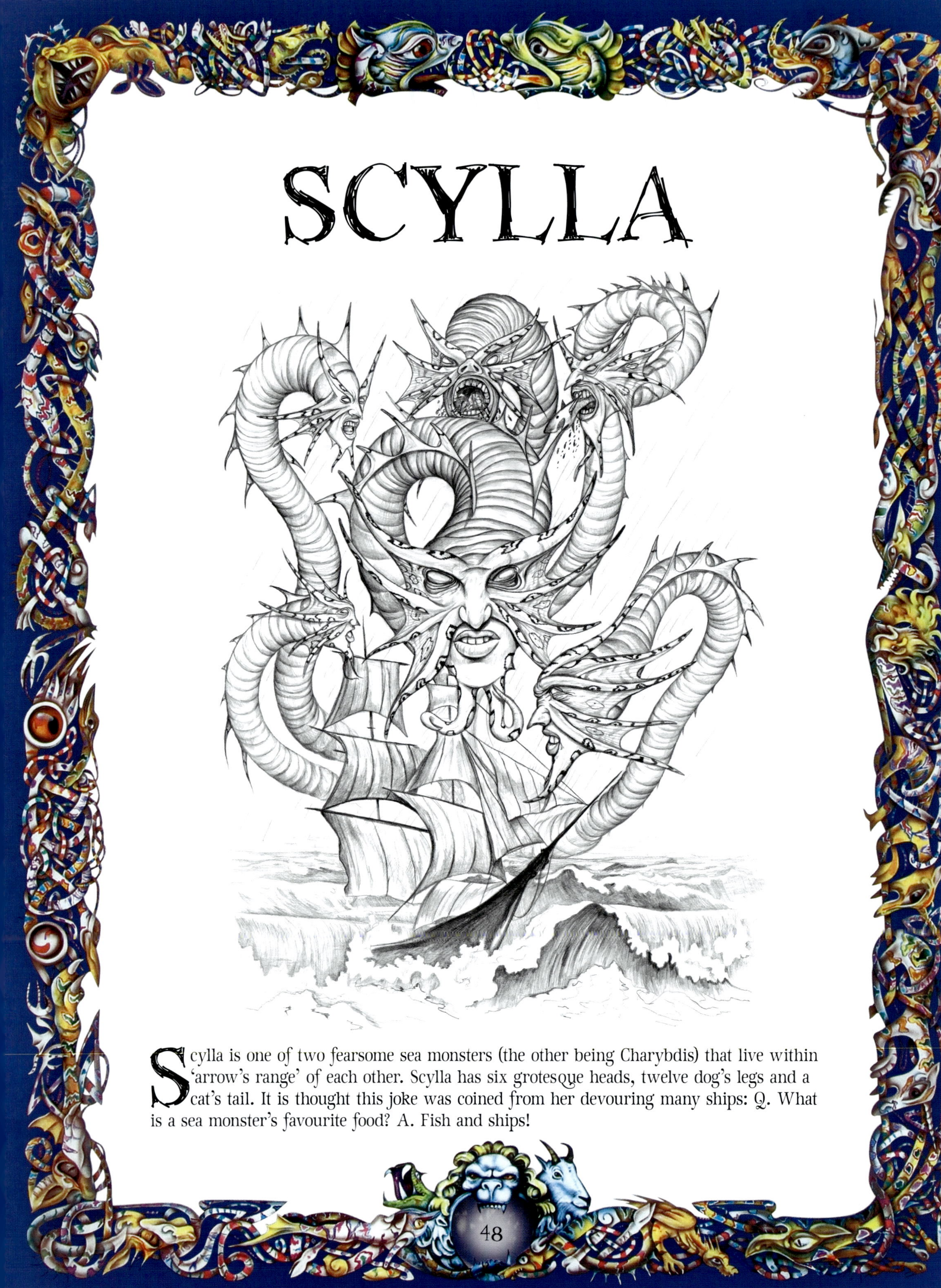

SCYLLA

Scylla is one of two fearsome sea monsters (the other being Charybdis) that live within 'arrow's range' of each other. Scylla has six grotesque heads, twelve dog's legs and a cat's tail. It is thought this joke was coined from her devouring many ships: Q. What is a sea monster's favourite food? A. Fish and ships!

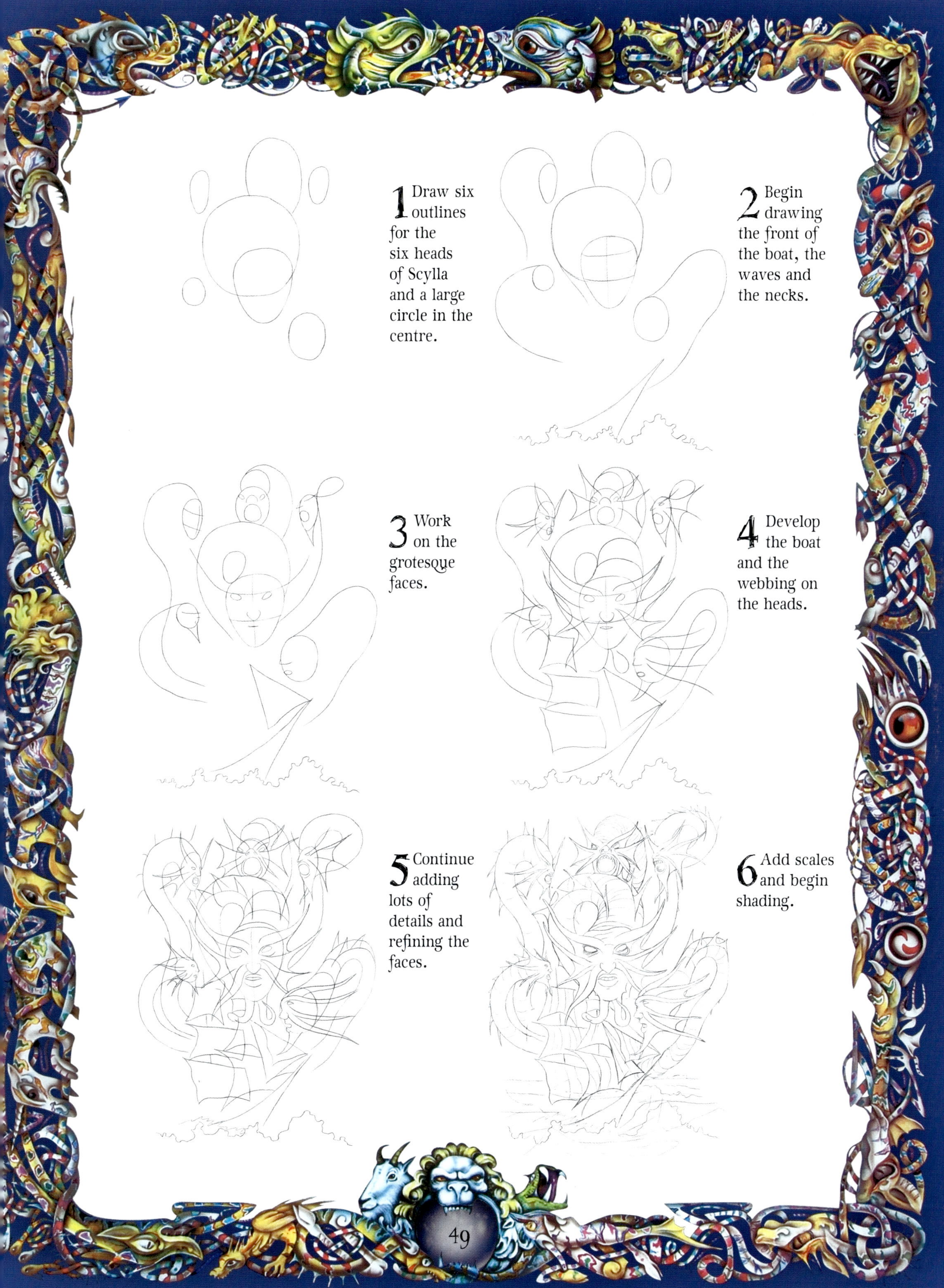

1 Draw six outlines for the six heads of Scylla and a large circle in the centre.

2 Begin drawing the front of the boat, the waves and the necks.

3 Work on the grotesque faces.

4 Develop the boat and the webbing on the heads.

5 Continue adding lots of details and refining the faces.

6 Add scales and begin shading.

CHARYBDIS

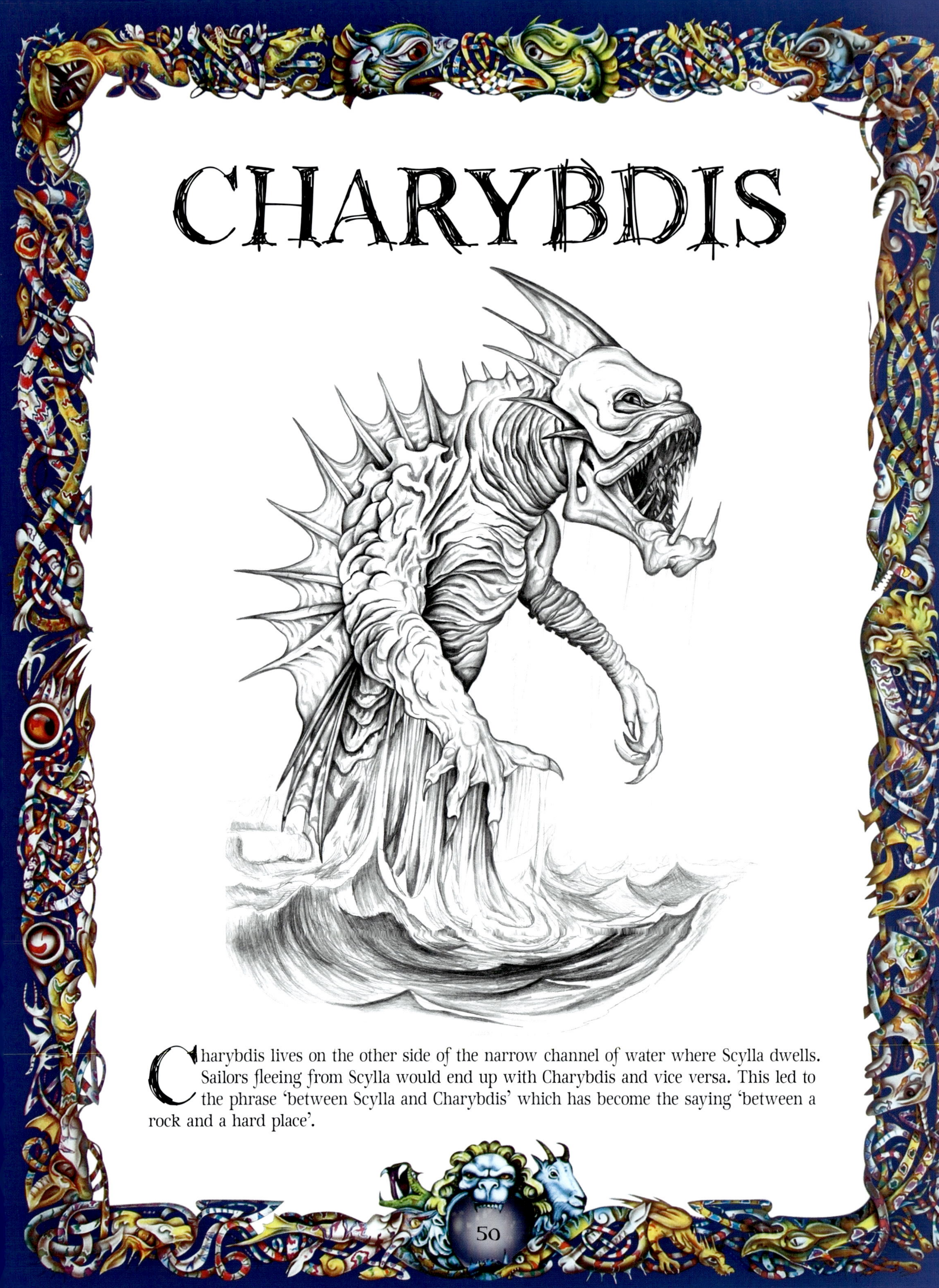

Charybdis lives on the other side of the narrow channel of water where Scylla dwells. Sailors fleeing from Scylla would end up with Charybdis and vice versa. This led to the phrase 'between Scylla and Charybdis' which has become the saying 'between a rock and a hard place'.

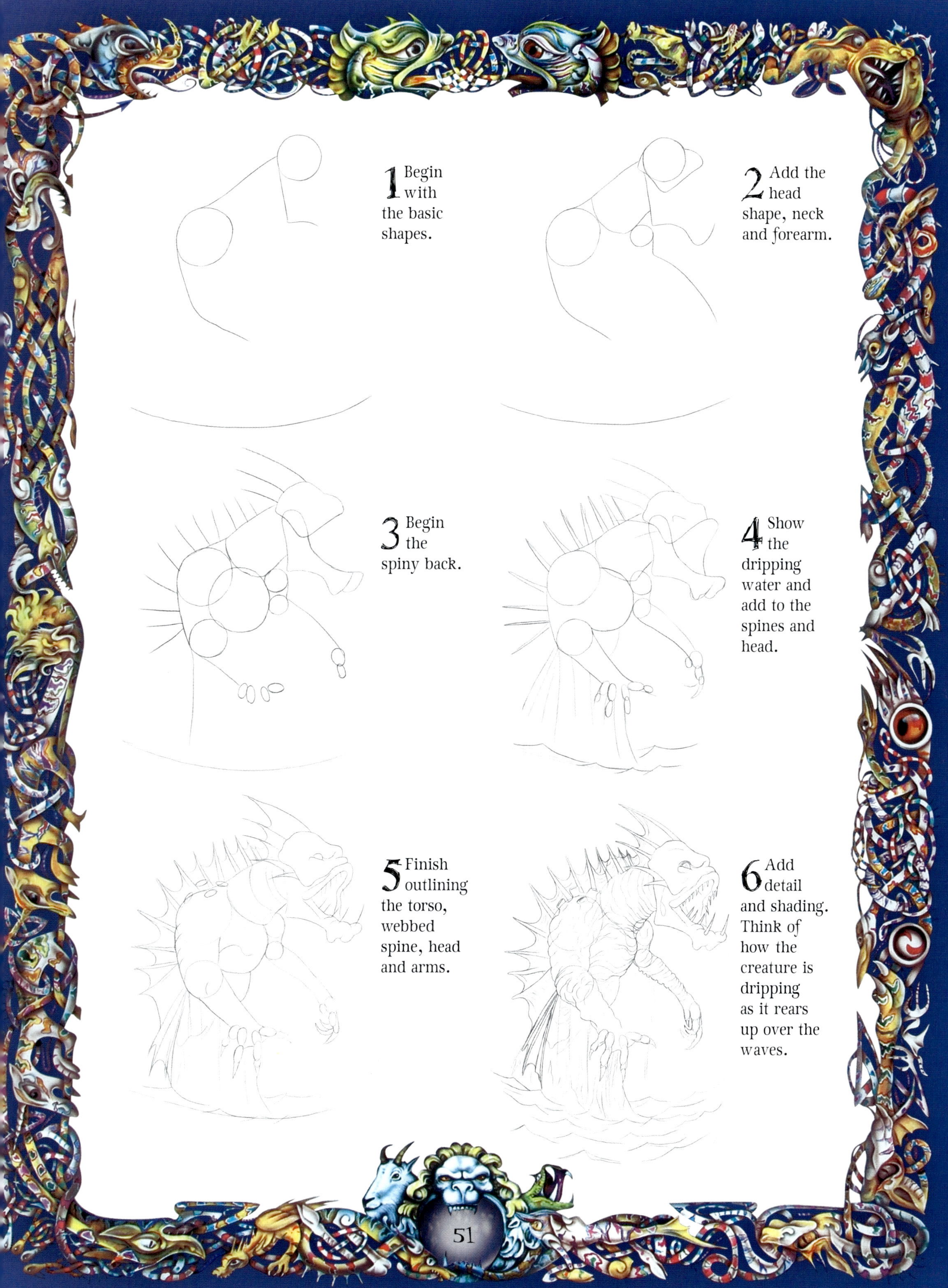
1 Begin with the basic shapes.
2 Add the head shape, neck and forearm.
3 Begin the spiny back.
4 Show the dripping water and add to the spines and head.
5 Finish outlining the torso, webbed spine, head and arms.
6 Add detail and shading. Think of how the creature is dripping as it rears up over the waves.

HYDRA

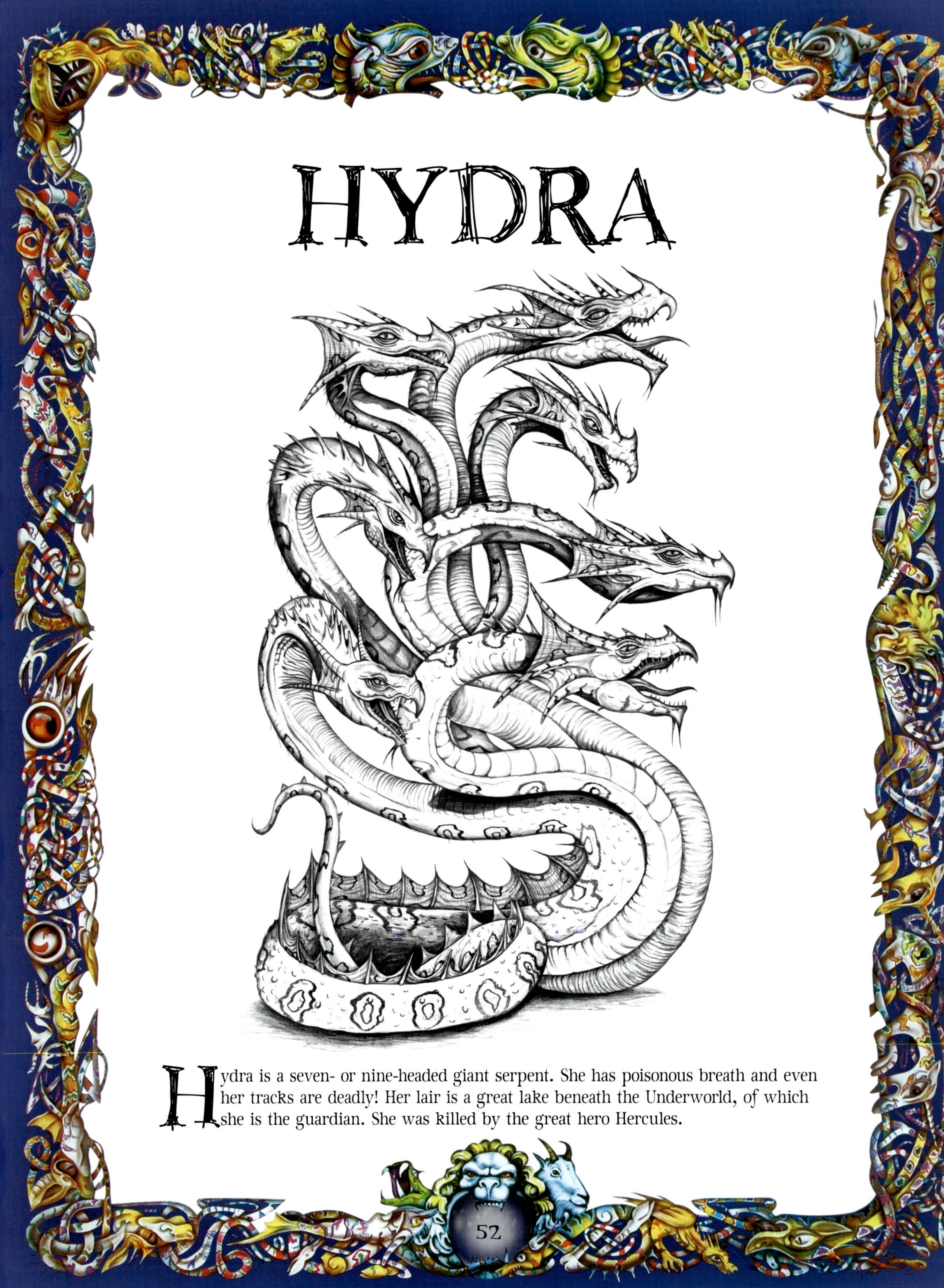

Hydra is a seven- or nine-headed giant serpent. She has poisonous breath and even her tracks are deadly! Her lair is a great lake beneath the Underworld, of which she is the guardian. She was killed by the great hero Hercules.

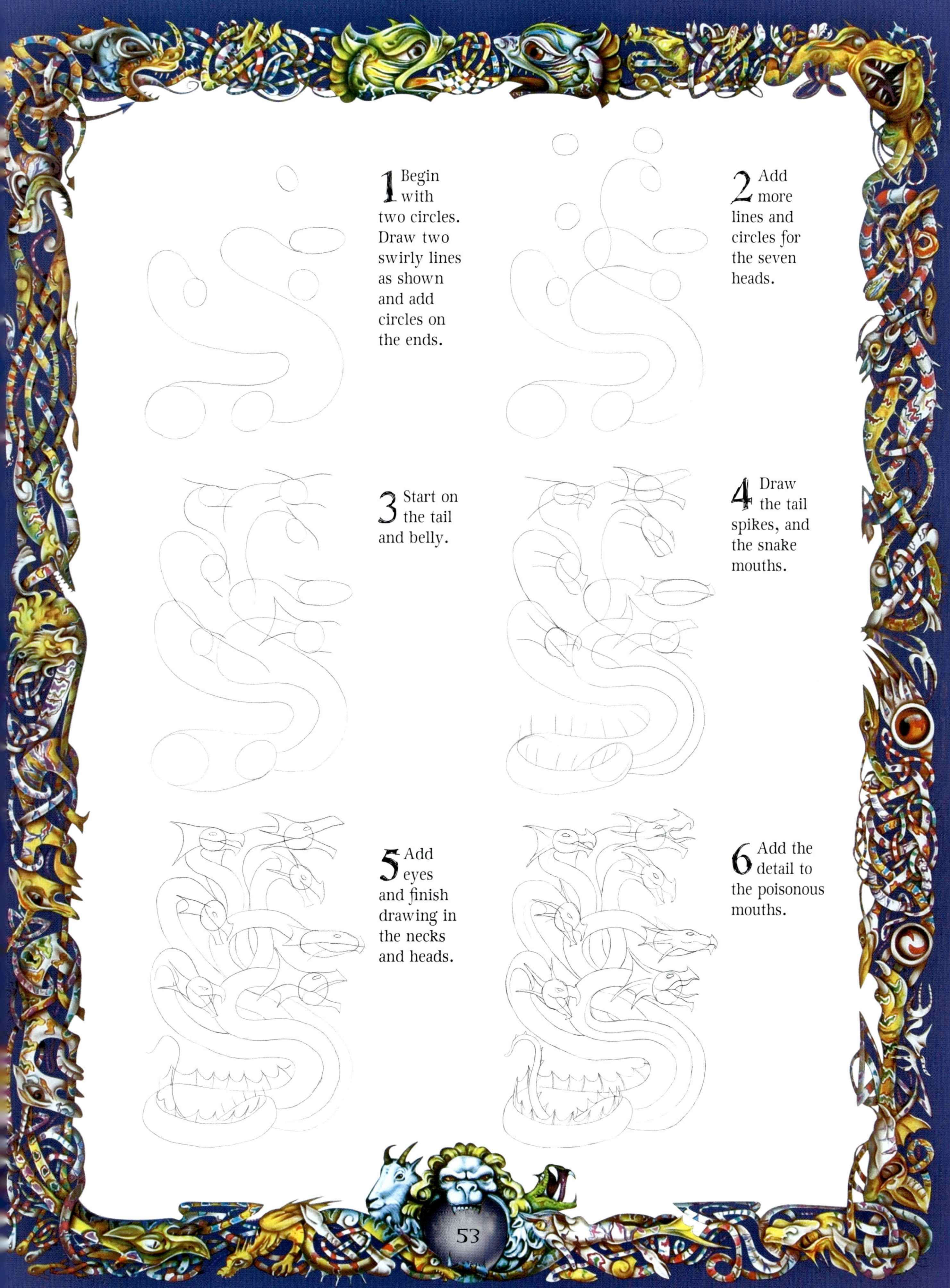

1 Begin with two circles. Draw two swirly lines as shown and add circles on the ends.

2 Add more lines and circles for the seven heads.

3 Start on the tail and belly.

4 Draw the tail spikes, and the snake mouths.

5 Add eyes and finish drawing in the necks and heads.

6 Add the detail to the poisonous mouths.

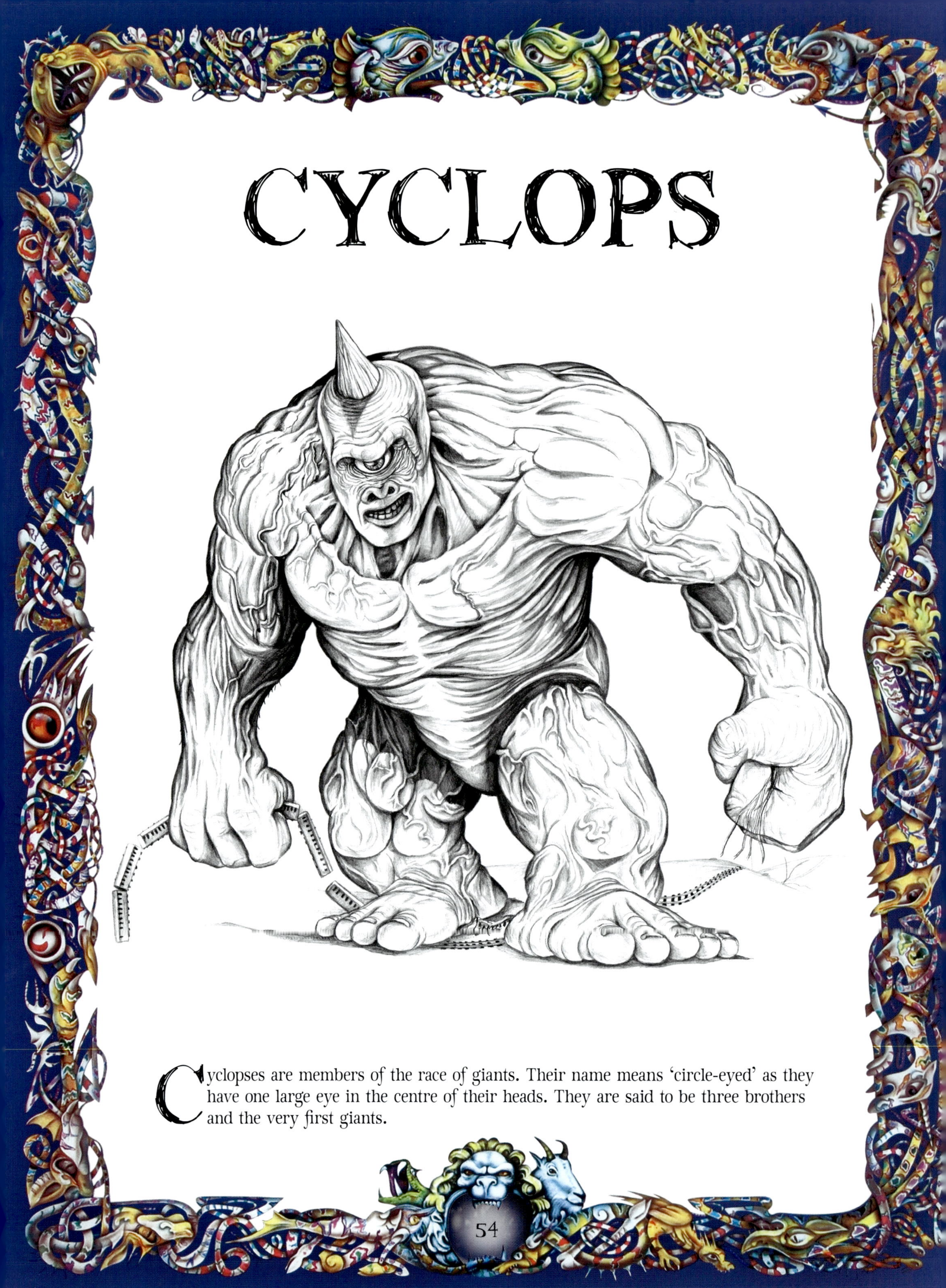

CYCLOPS

Cyclopses are members of the race of giants. Their name means 'circle-eyed' as they have one large eye in the centre of their heads. They are said to be three brothers and the very first giants.

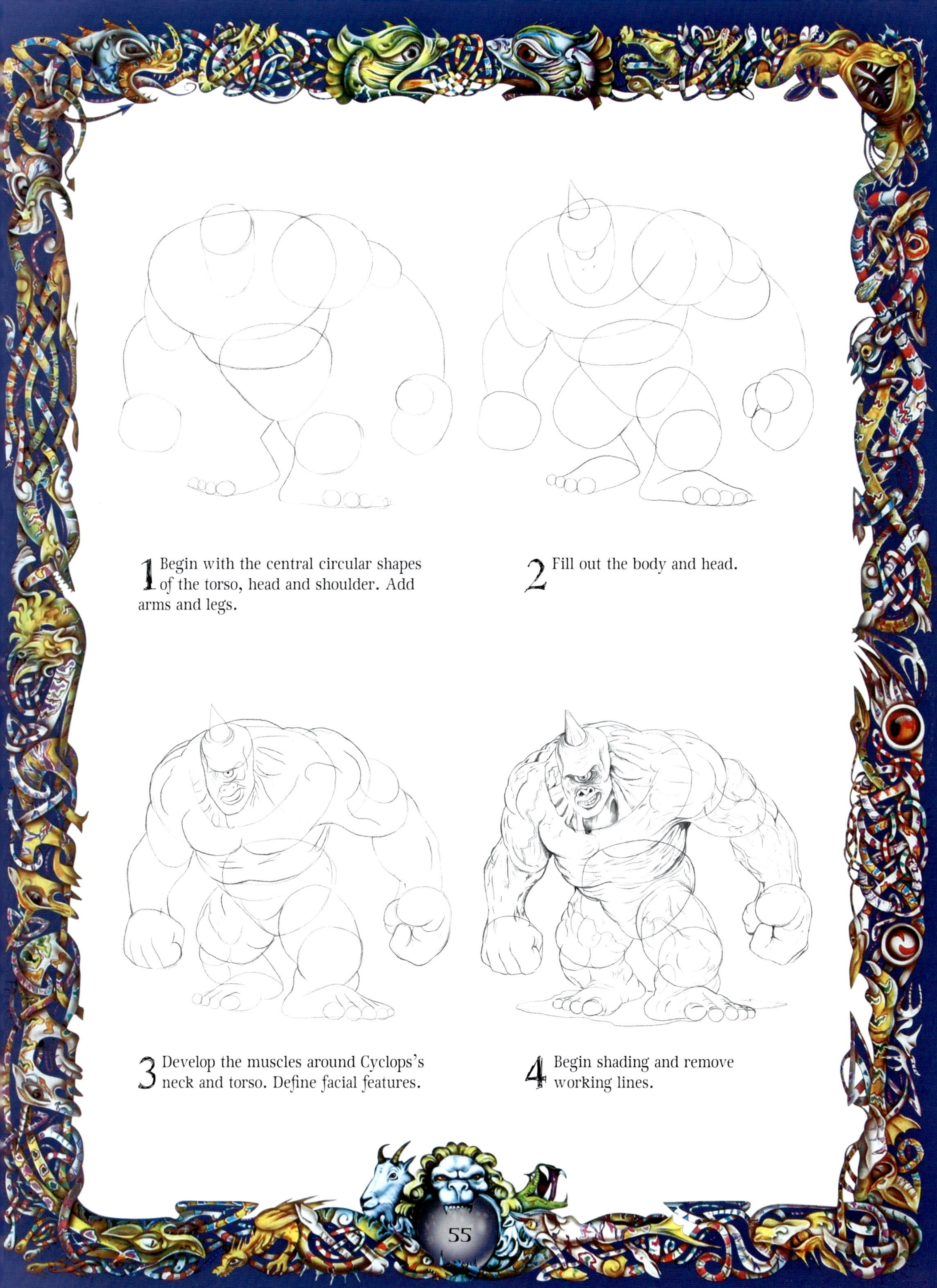

1 Begin with the central circular shapes of the torso, head and shoulder. Add arms and legs.

2 Fill out the body and head.

3 Develop the muscles around Cyclops's neck and torso. Define facial features.

4 Begin shading and remove working lines.

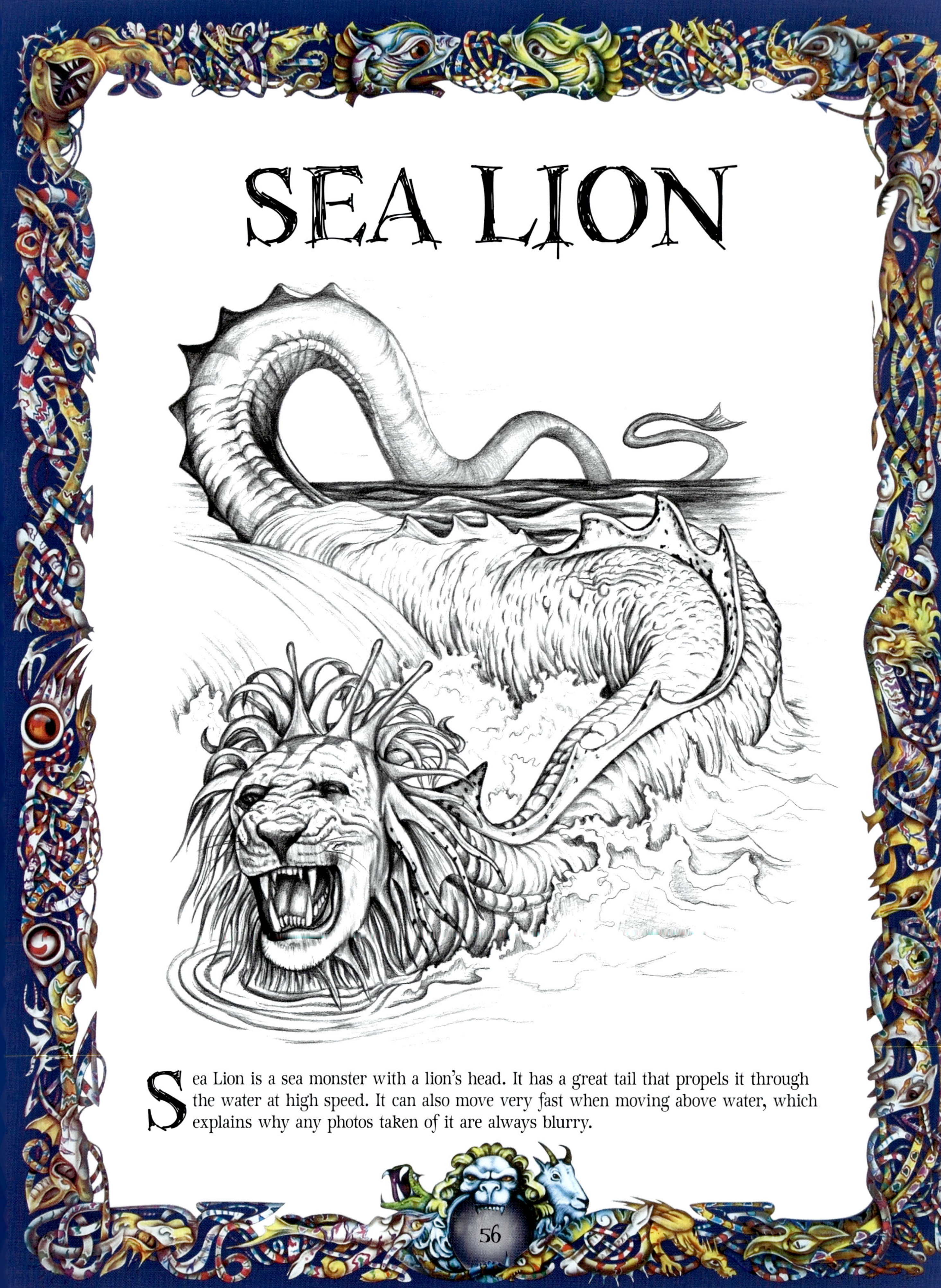

SEA LION

Sea Lion is a sea monster with a lion's head. It has a great tail that propels it through the water at high speed. It can also move very fast when moving above water, which explains why any photos taken of it are always blurry.

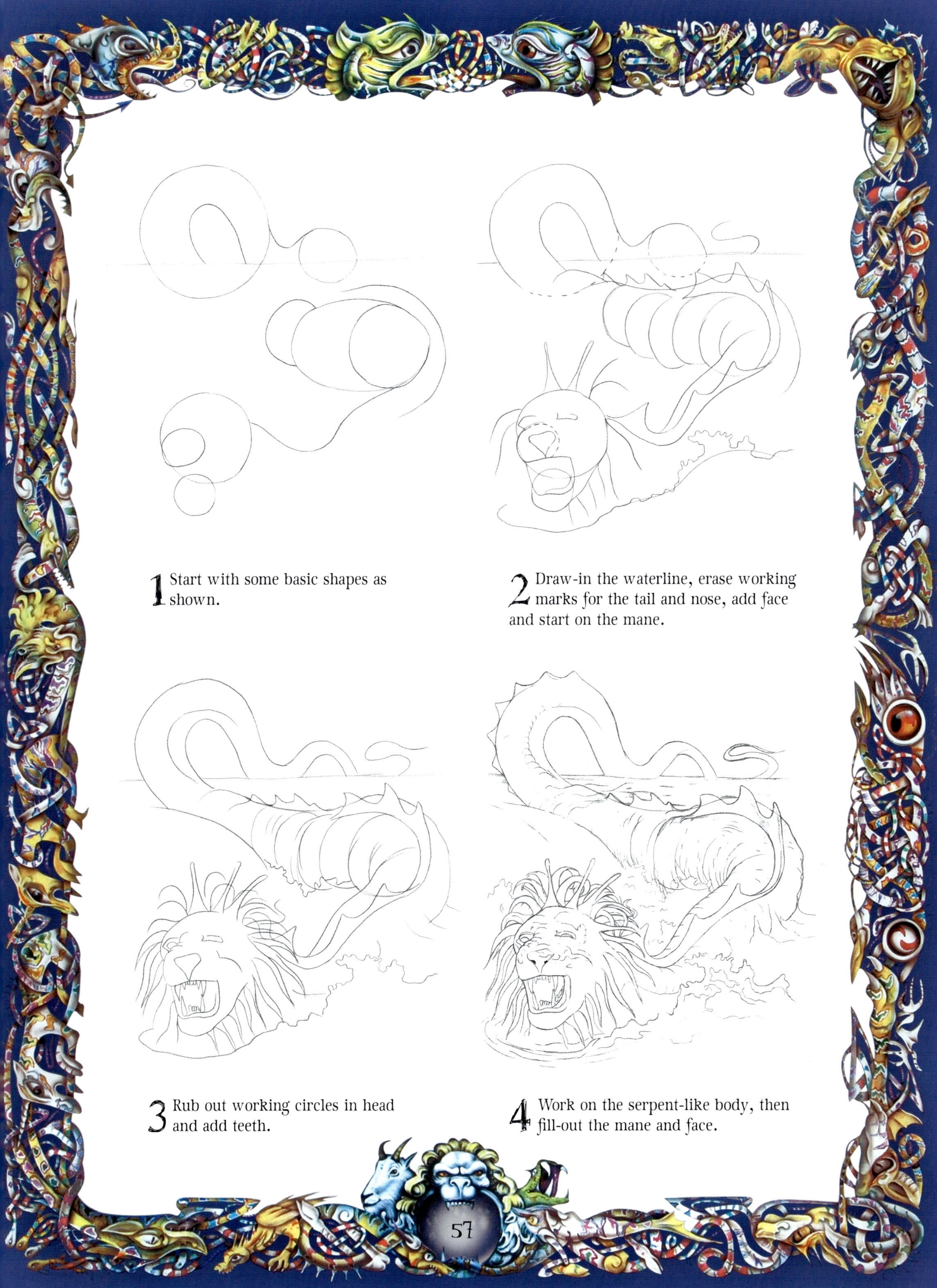

1 Start with some basic shapes as shown.

2 Draw-in the waterline, erase working marks for the tail and nose, add face and start on the mane.

3 Rub out working circles in head and add teeth.

4 Work on the serpent-like body, then fill-out the mane and face.

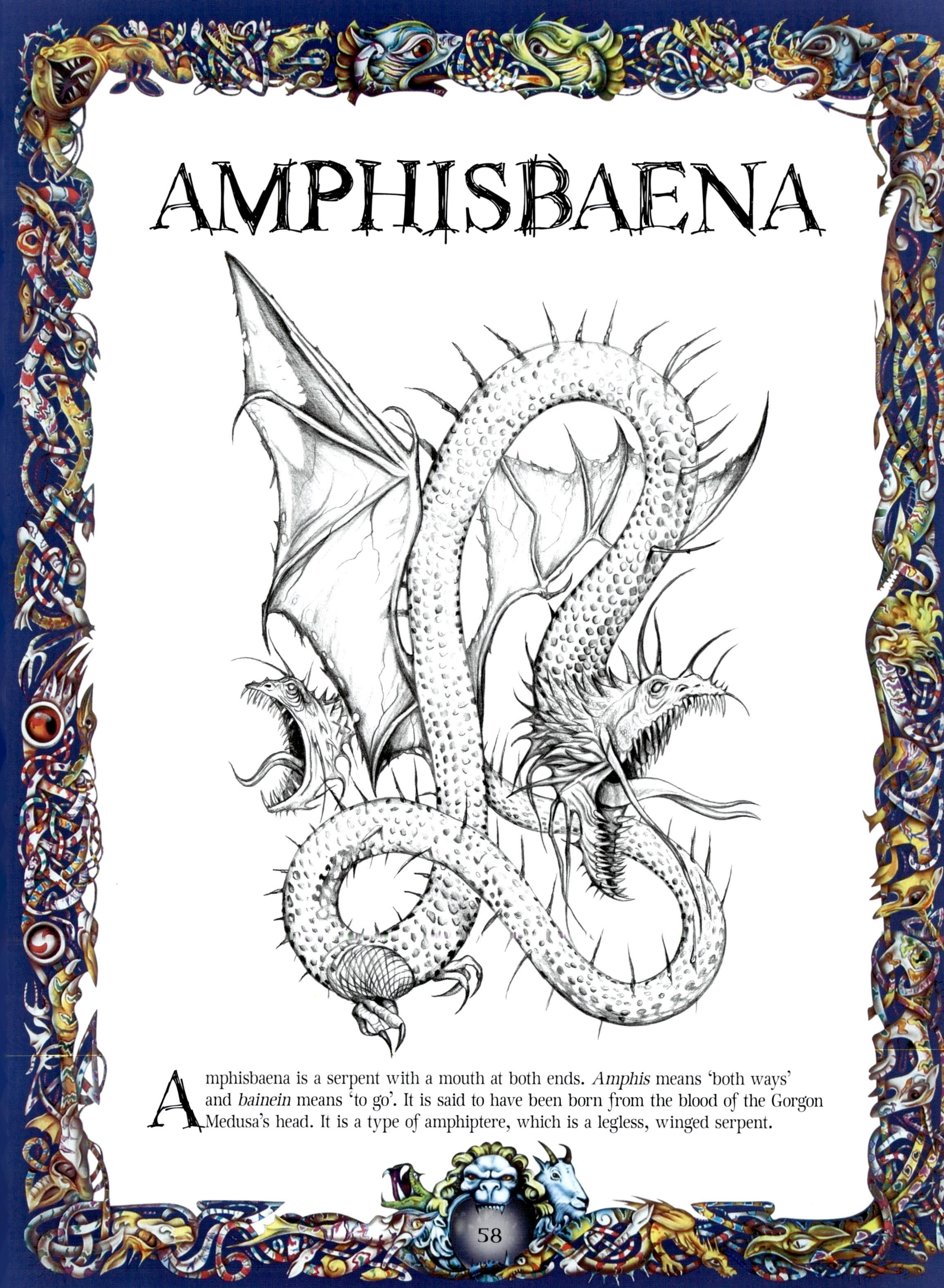

AMPHISBAENA

Amphisbaena is a serpent with a mouth at both ends. *Amphis* means 'both ways' and *bainein* means 'to go'. It is said to have been born from the blood of the Gorgon Medusa's head. It is a type of amphiptere, which is a legless, winged serpent.

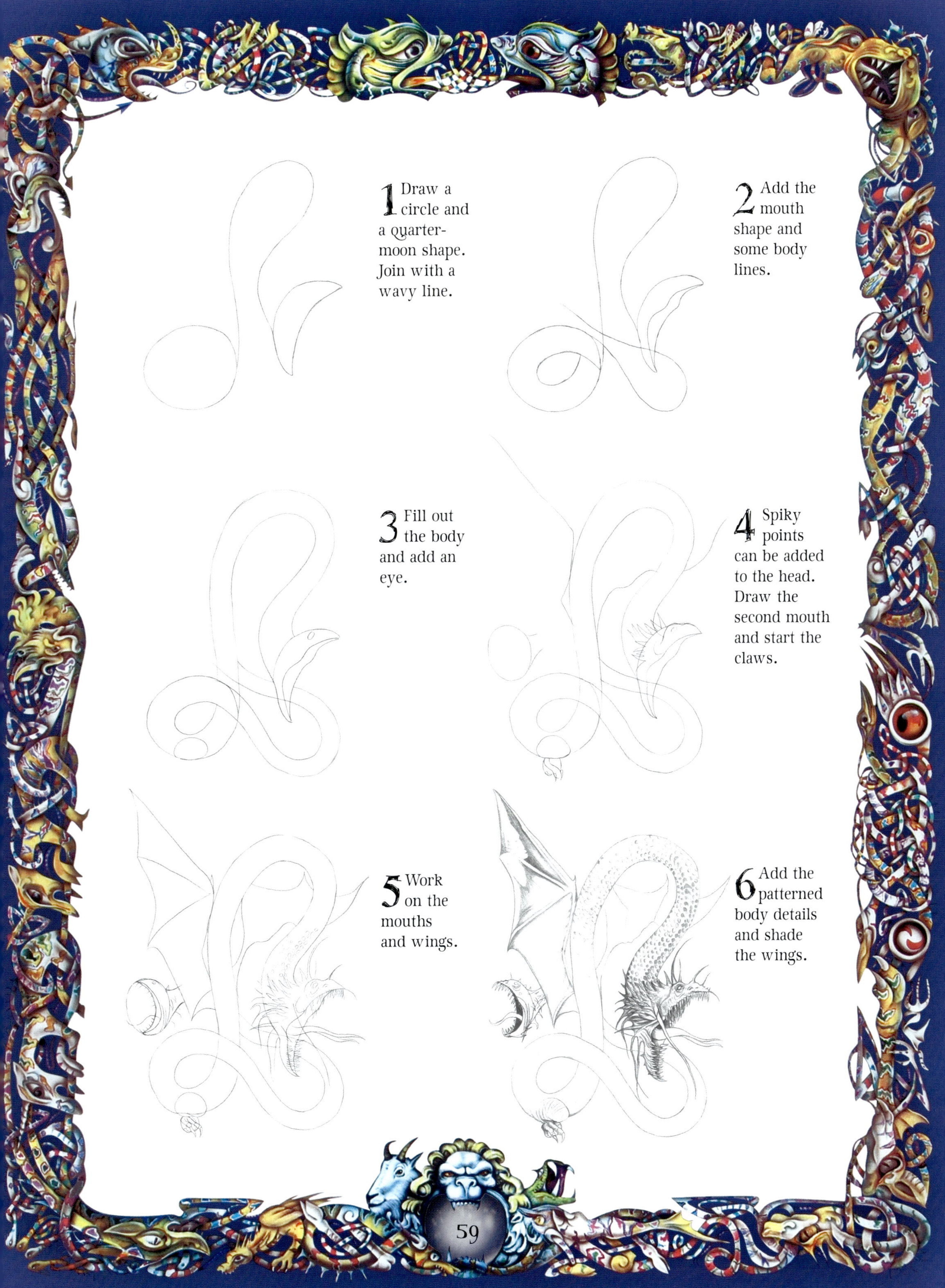

1 Draw a circle and a quarter-moon shape. Join with a wavy line.

2 Add the mouth shape and some body lines.

3 Fill out the body and add an eye.

4 Spiky points can be added to the head. Draw the second mouth and start the claws.

5 Work on the mouths and wings.

6 Add the patterned body details and shade the wings.

KRAKEN

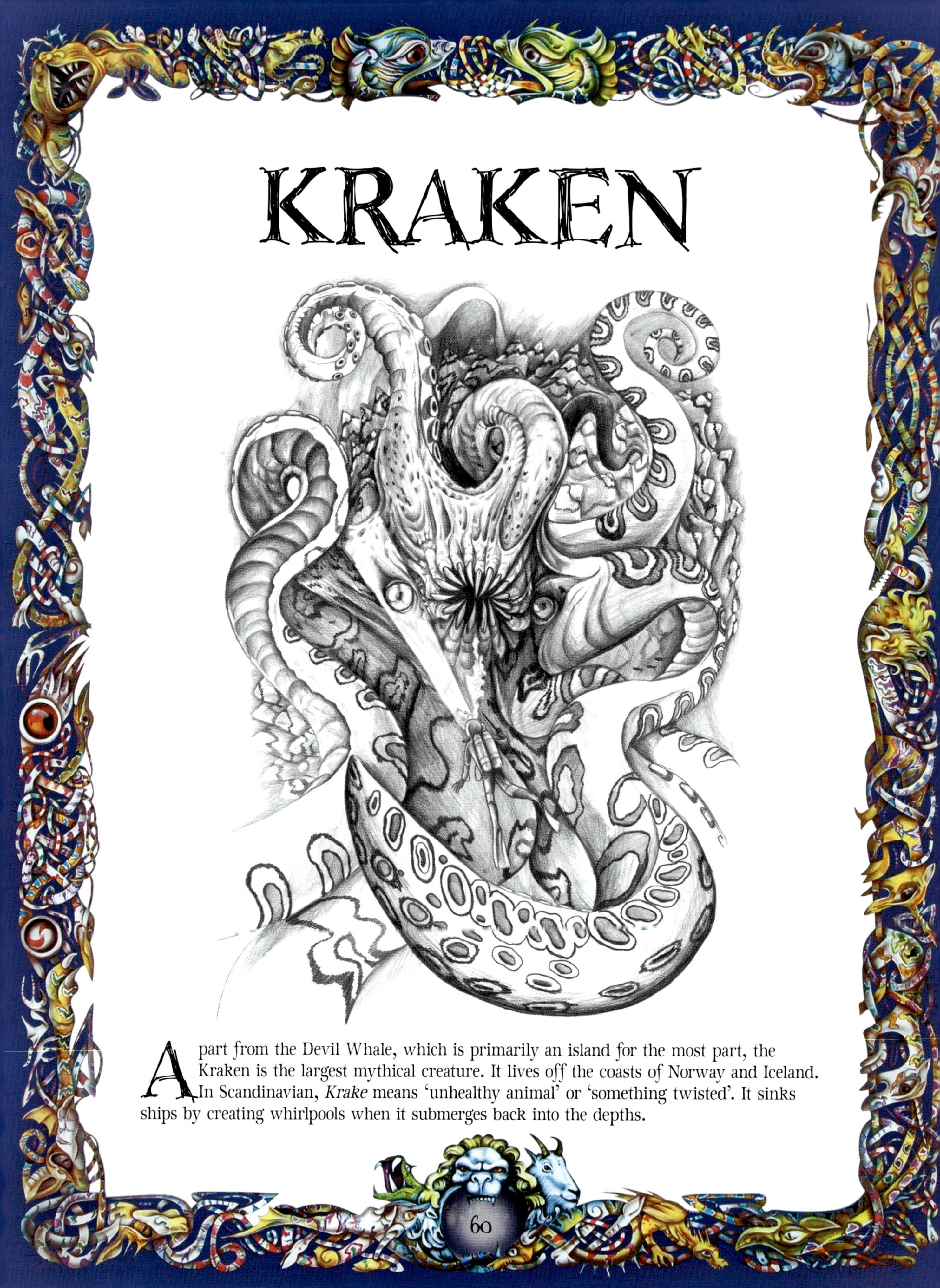

Apart from the Devil Whale, which is primarily an island for the most part, the Kraken is the largest mythical creature. It lives off the coasts of Norway and Iceland. In Scandinavian, *Krake* means 'unhealthy animal' or 'something twisted'. It sinks ships by creating whirlpools when it submerges back into the depths.

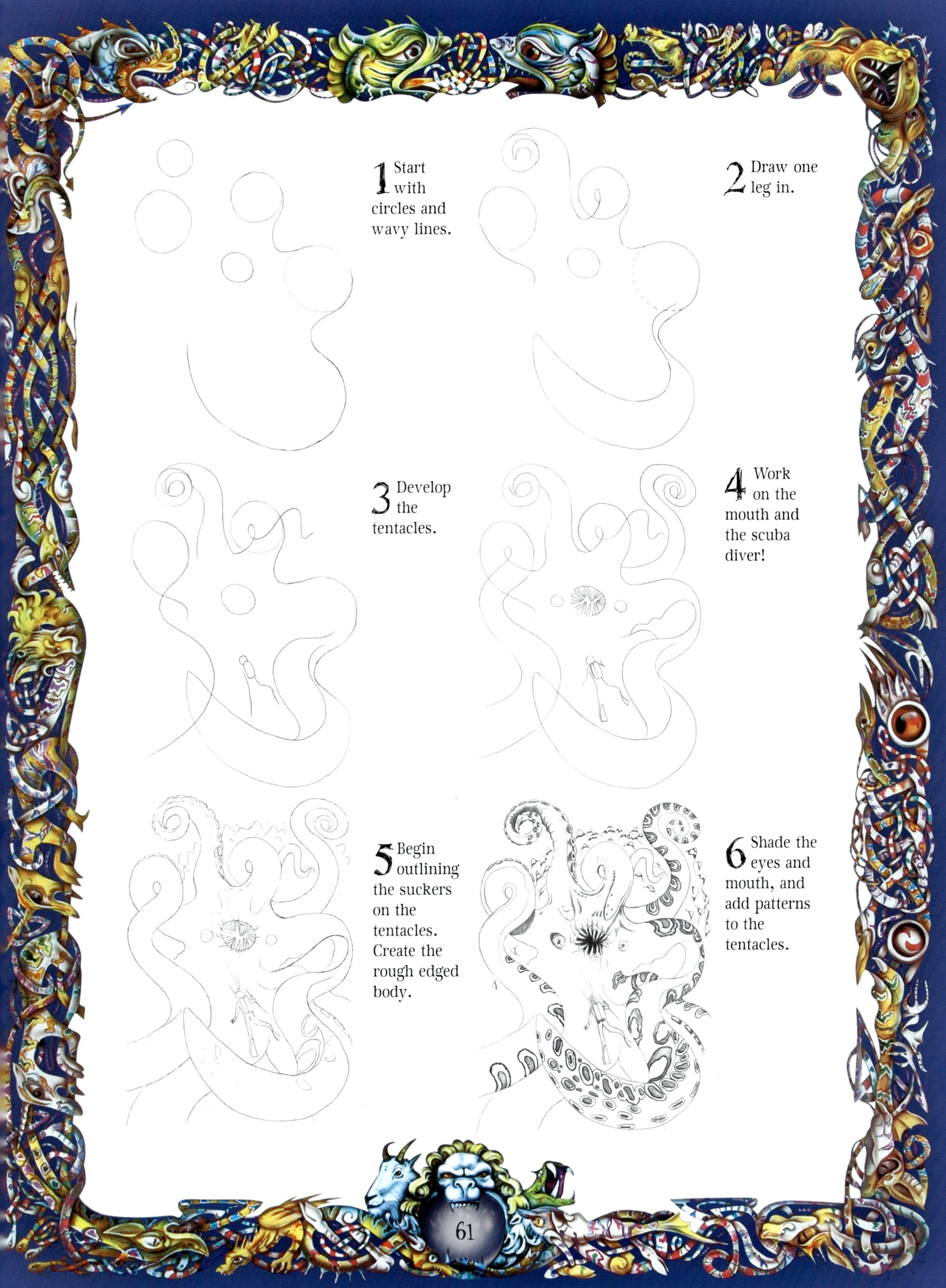

1 Start with circles and wavy lines.

2 Draw one leg in.

3 Develop the tentacles.

4 Work on the mouth and the scuba diver!

5 Begin outlining the suckers on the tentacles. Create the rough edged body.

6 Shade the eyes and mouth, and add patterns to the tentacles.

MYTHICAL LETTERING

Finish off your drawings with mythical lettering styles.
Try these or make up your own!

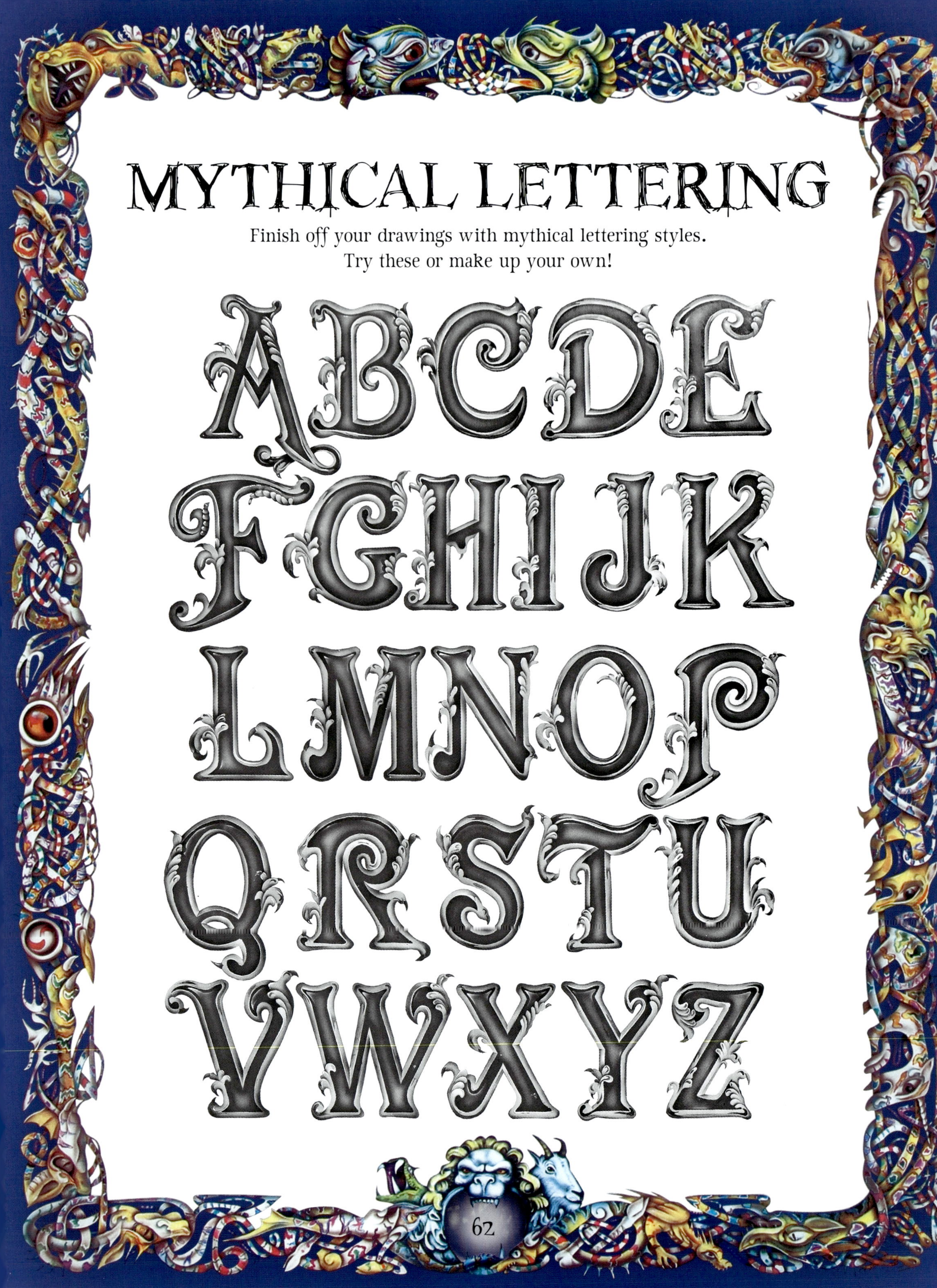

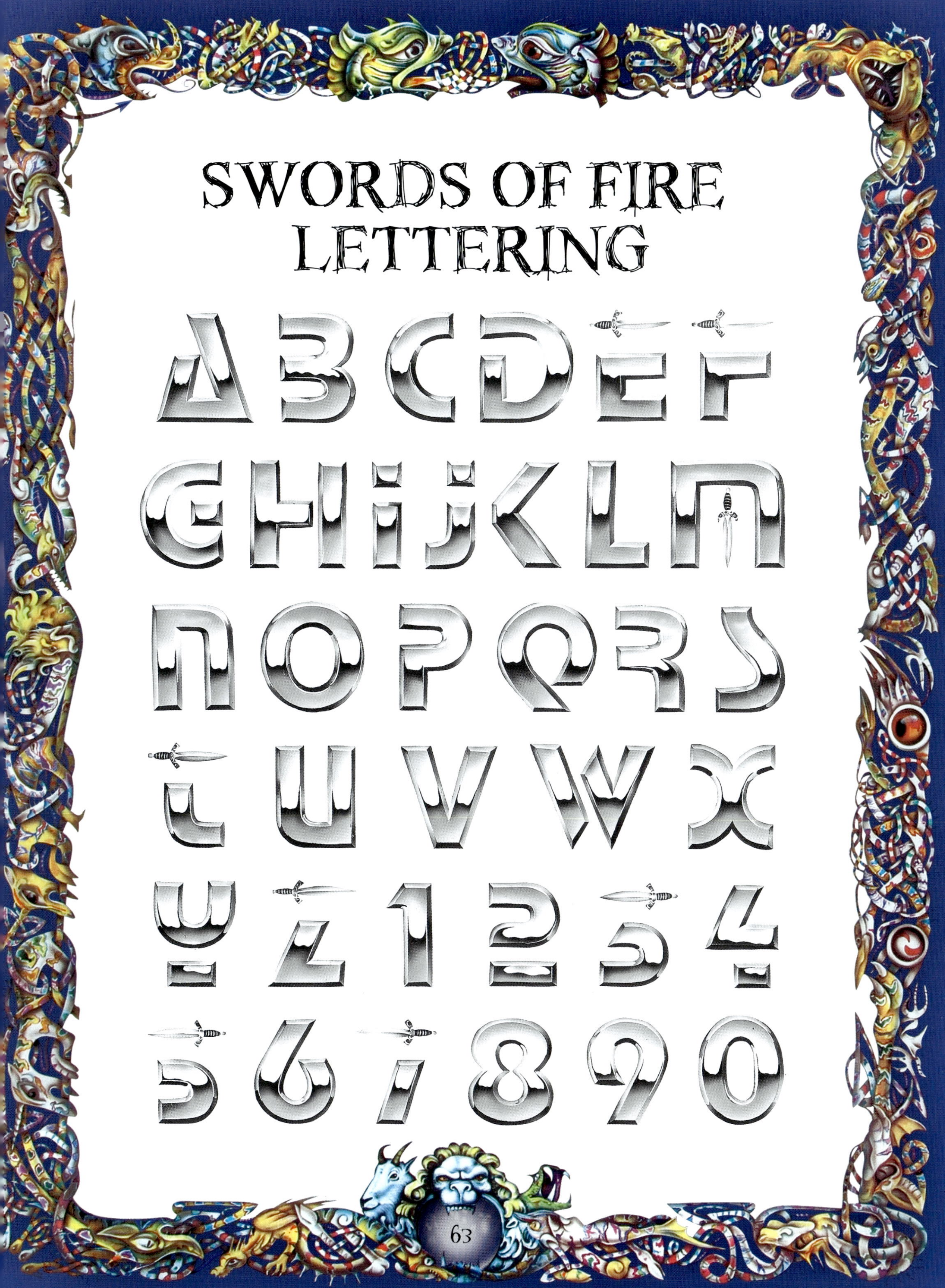
SWORDS OF FIRE
LETTERING
ABCDEF
GHIJKLM
NOPQRS
TUVWX
YZ1234
567890

MYTHICAL CREATURES AT SCHOOL!

Work out which of these creatures you'd like to take to school for show and tell, for lunch (just be careful if they decide your classmates ARE lunch) or as one of the student body! Choose your creature by comparing their mythical abilities (M) and if they'd be a good student (S)! Peaceful = Purple, Fierce = Teal, Very Dangerous = Orange

SPHINX

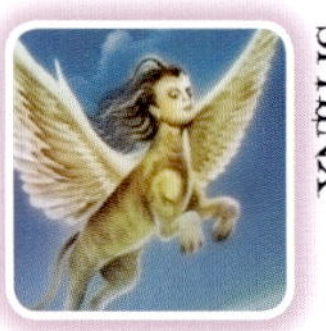

M: Guards temples
S: Good at Egyptian studies

GORGON

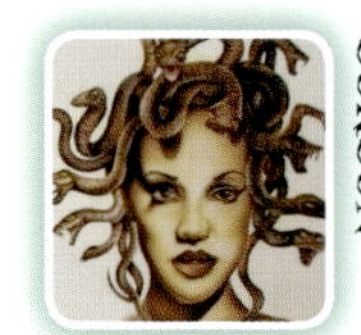

M: Likes snakes
S: Turns class to stone

LINDWORM

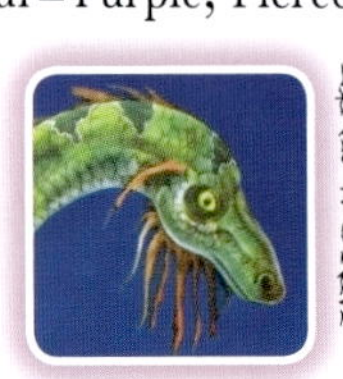

M: Fast mover
S: Good in soccer team

SATYR

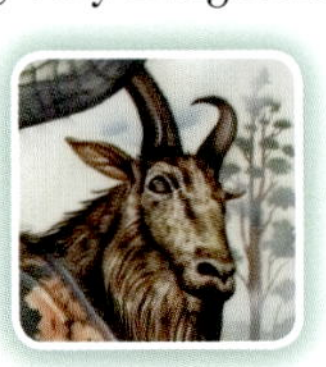

M: Creates merriment
S: Lots of fun, no work

GRIFFIN

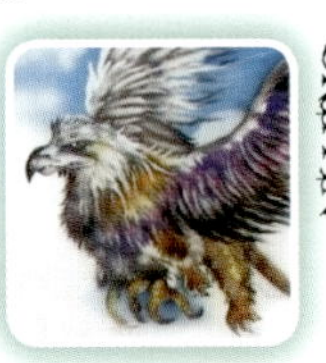

M: A flying lion!
S: Secretive (no copying homework!)

CYCLOPS

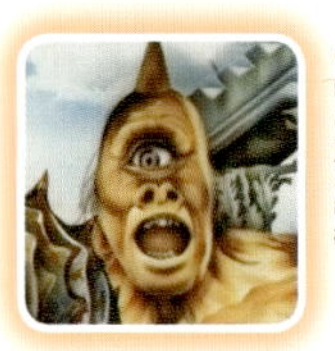

M: One-eyed giant
S: Intense stare = awkward!

PHOENIX

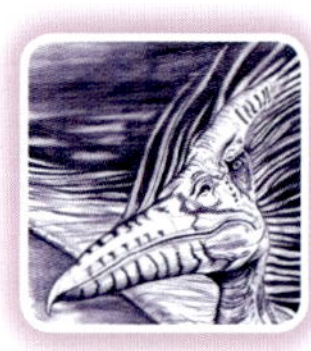

M: Long life span
S: Could burst into flames

AMMIT

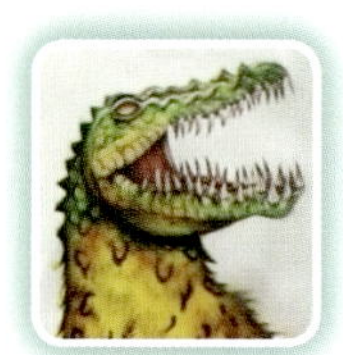

M: Good doer
S: Volunteers you for cleaning duty

SEA LION

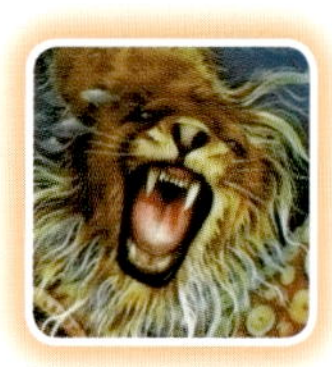

M: Fast in water
S: Always blurry in school photos

PEGASUS

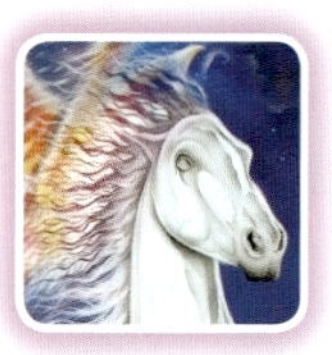

M: Flies
S: Pegasus rides at lunch time?

HARPY

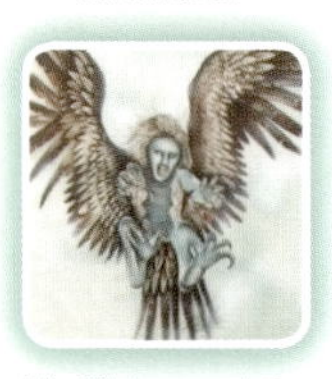

M: Flying snatcher
S: Bad at thumb wrestling

AMPHISBAENA

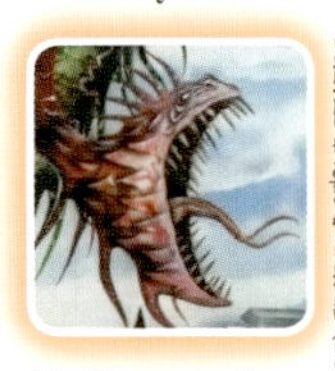

M: Two mouths
S: Detention for biting!

FAIRY

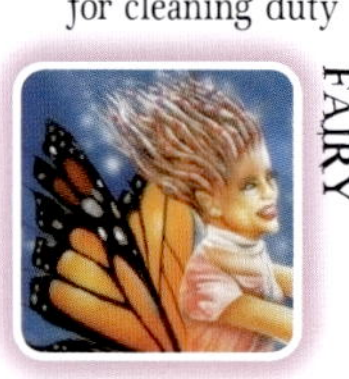

M: Magical powers
S: Easily lost due to size

CHARYBDIS

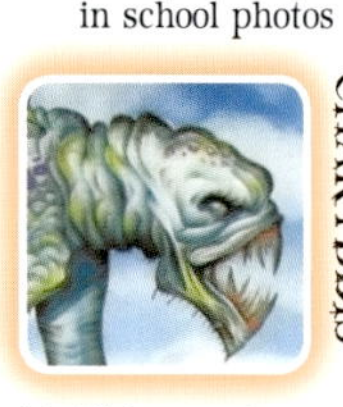

M: Fish monster
S: Only interested in marine studies

PYRAUSTA

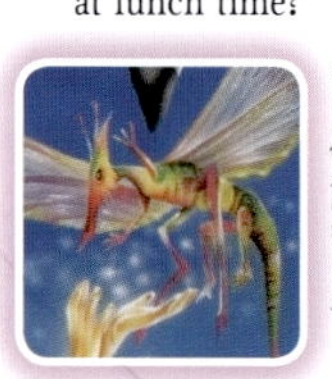

M: 'Borrows' stationery
S: Could be taught to 'borrow' lunch?

DEVIL WHALE

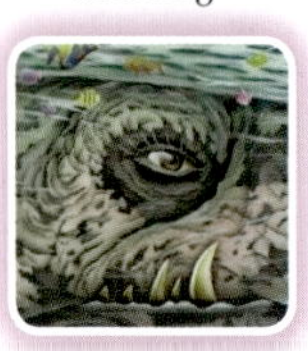

M: Mind-bogglingly enormous
S: Could make whole school disappear!

CERBERUS

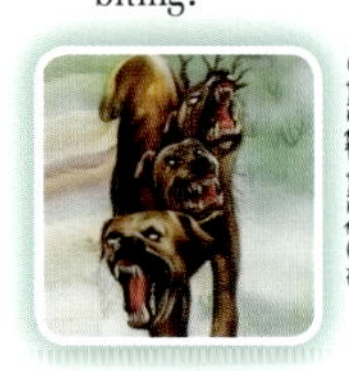

M: Guard dog
S: Not toilet trained

KRAKEN

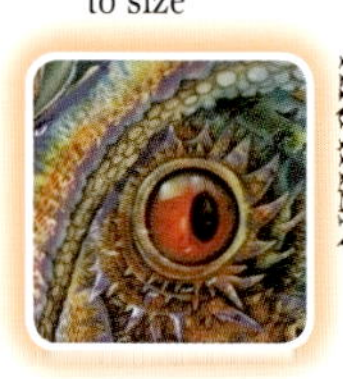

M: Creates whirlpools
S: Fills entire auditorium = no assembly!

MERMAID

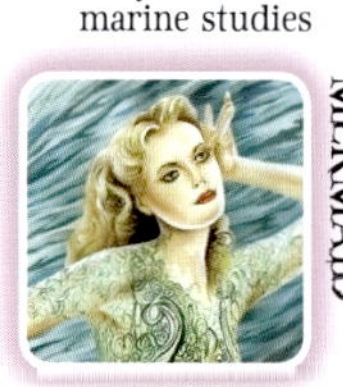

M: Good singers and swimmers
S: Excellent in the swimming team!

CENTAUR

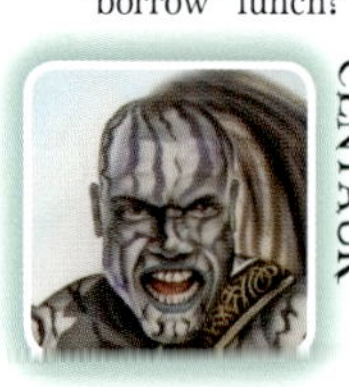

M: Teacher/Warrior
S: Commandeers history class

MINOTAUR

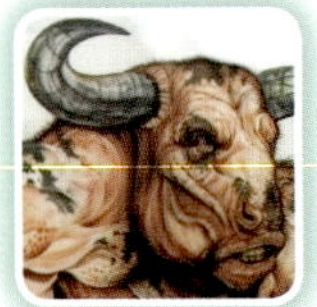

M: Not very good at mazes
S: Good in canteen line

HYDRA

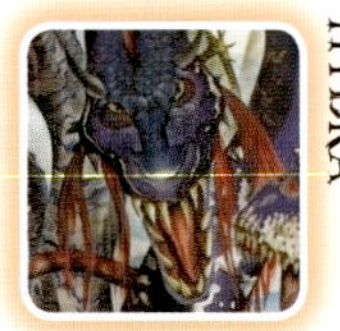

M: Poisonous breath
S: Can watch your back . . . from all angles!

CHIMERA

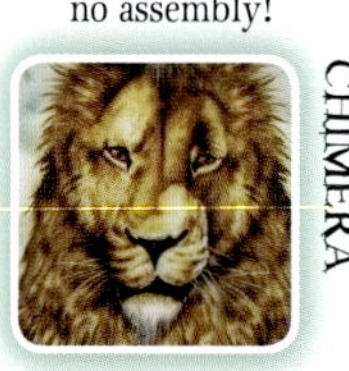

M: Fire-breathing
S: Giggle-inducing

UNICORN

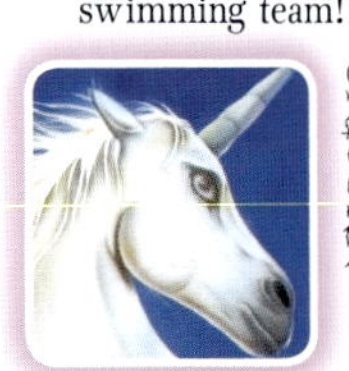

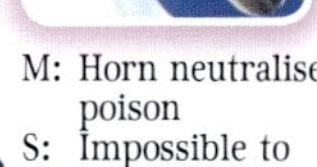

M: Horn neutralises poison
S: Impossible to tame = wilful!

SCYLLA

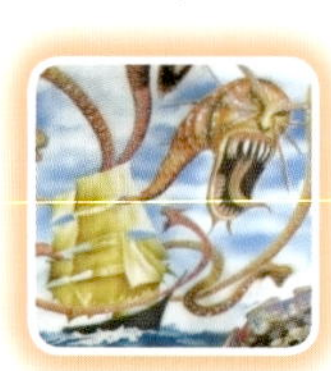

M: Eats ships
S: Not chips, SHIPS! (OK, will make do with rowing team)